The
Wilderness
Notebook

The Wilderness Notebook

Herb Gordon

BURFORD BOOKS

Dedicated to
Sande
and to those
once-upon-a-time kids—
Cary, Deborah, Hilary, and Rebecca—
who brought laughter to the wilderness.

Printed in the United States of America.
10 9 8 7 6 5 4 3 2 1
Library of Congress Cataloging-in-Publication Data

Gordon, Herb.
    The wilderness notebook / by Herb Gordon.
        p.   cm.
    Includes index.
    ISBN 1-58080-033-5 (pbk.)
    1. Camping—Handbooks, manuals, etc. 2. Camping—Equip-
ment and supplies—Handbooks, manuals, etc. 3. Outdoor
recreation—Handbooks, manuals, etc. 4. Wilderness survival—
Handbooks, manuals, etc.   I. Title.
GV191.7.G678   1999
796.54—dc21   99-11945
                                                       CIP

Contents

Introduction

I went into the woods because I wished to live deliberately, to front only the essential facts of life, and see if I could not learn what it had to teach, and not, when I came to die, discover that I had not lived.
—Henry David Thoreau
  1817–1862

In truth, after backpacking and canoeing, rock climbing and day hiking, car camping and mountain (on easy dirt roads) biking for more than 50 years I still accept how I felt as a kid climbing the sagebrush-covered foothills in the towering mountains above my home in Pocatello for our weekend backpacking safaris: I'm a lazy outdoorsperson.

An easier way to do something? Show me. A better way to do something else? I learn quickly. A smart way to avoid a stupid problem? Thanks for the advice. A technique I never thought of? Good! A bit of new knowledge about the outdoors? Why didn't I know that? A reminder of something long unremembered? How could I have forgotten?

There is, for example, how the wise canoeist sets up an excellent worktable in the wilderness without strain. I'd been paddling a few years before I learned it.

It happened on a weeklong canoe trip on the Allagash Wilderness Waterway, which winds across the magnificent forests of northern Maine, where I was leading a group of eight teenagers. We had been paddling on a beautiful late-summer day with a pleasant tailwind. No one had a word of complaint about the conditions as we dug our blades into the waters, heading toward our preplanned camp area.

My lead canoe swung around a point of land and stopped. The bow paddler raised her hand and motioned for me. I paddled over.

"Look." She pointed toward the campsite. It had an outdoor fireplace, an open shelter cabin, camp table, and benches. Occupied! A half-dozen campers, canoes pulled up on shore, waved to us. This was the first time since our trip began three days ago that a group was already in the campsite we had been paddling toward.

"Oh, damn. What'll we do now?" her stern paddler, a tall, soft-spoken, and muscular young fellow, asked.

"Go ashore. There's lots of room to set up our tents," I said. We paddled to the beach, pulled up the canoes, and set about organizing our own camp at a cleared area nearby with a couple of fire rings. But no shelter, table, or fireplace.

Almost as our last tents were set up, another two canoes rounded the bend and headed for shore. They in turn set up their camp at another fire ring a short distance from ours.

Within the hour, our three groups were mingling, exchanging goodwill and "where'd-you-come-froms."

And then I saw something startling. The four latest arrivals had something we didn't—a "table" for their kitchen. They had hauled one canoe to their camp area, tipped it upside-down, and placed two flat logs under the bow and stern decks to keep it firm and steady—and lo! A table. I've been ever grateful to those Allagash friends who taught me how to be more comfortable in a wilderness camp—when you have a canoe along.

Over the years I've picked up an ongoing supply of good ideas from others on the trail and in camps, and from what wilderness veterans have written, that have been a pleasure to know whether backpacking the Sawtooth Mountains or making a family camp in the Adirondacks—even to such bits of advice as my Scoutmaster of decades ago stressed: "Keep your knife sharp. It'll work better."

And that's the motif of this wilderness notebook. Read. Enjoy. You may pick up a helpful tip or two that will make your next wilderness adventure, whether afoot or on horseback, via canoe or mountain bike, on snowshoes or skis, "work better."

1

Getting Physical

Up lad; when the journey's over
There'll be time enough to sleep.
  —Alfred E. Housman
    1859–1936

So your goal this summer is a great adventure in a seagoing kayak with an outfit that will spend two weeks paddling coastal waters of Alaska. Or high mountain biking in California's Lake Tahoe country. Maybe backpacking for two weeks on the Appalachian Trail where it climbs up and down several thousand feet a day as it crosses the Great Smokies.

Dr. Wade Johnson, a New York internist, recommends that you be physically prepared before leaping off on a journey that requires a healthy, sturdy body. No matter what your age.

A Basic Fitness Program

Dr. Johnson says the basic preparation for any wilderness adventure is a couple of months of physical conditioning for those of us whose usual greatest activity is an occasional long walk through the park, or from the car to the mall.

A regimen he suggests includes, but is not limited to, three key elements at least four times a week: 1. aerobic exercises or jumping rope; or 2. briskly walking a couple of miles, working out on a treadmill, or swimming; and 3. using weights to strengthen the lower back and knees.

Specialized Programs for Outdoor Sports

In addition to the basics, here are exercises specifically recommended for your sport.

MOUNTAIN BIKING

The most common injuries in mountain biking, according to Dr. David Altchek at the Hospital for Special Surgery in Manhattan, are separated shoulders and clavicle fractures from falling over the handlebars. He said that those who strengthen their trunks have the best chance of not getting injured on a rough trail.

He recommended strengthening the upper body with weight pulldowns on a Nautilus machine, bench presses, and push-ups.

Keep in mind: Four times a week.

BACKPACKING

"Respiratory fitness" is a phrase often used to describe the key to mountaineering. The objective is to ready your lungs by regular exercise that stresses heavy breathing, such as short periods of hearty swimming or rope jumping.

It also is important for the backpacker to regularly exercise abdominal muscles, because the backpacking gear puts stress on the midsection.

Flexibility of feet and ankles is essential for backpackers who may be skipping lightly over wildflowers one moment, then slipping and sliding as they edge up a steep slope covered with scree. Here is one recommended series of daily exercises:

Sitting on a chair, straighten the knees to raise the feet. Circle each foot to the right 10 times, then 10 to the left. Point toes outward, then toward the body 10 times. Finally, stand on the balls of your feet, raise yourself as high as possible, and hold for a moment, then drop back on your heels. Repeat 10 times.

ROCK CLIMBING

Is this the year you are going to tackle climbing? Go for it. But go prepared.

The entire body must be in condition when your fingers stretch for bits of rock and your toes push you up the sheer rock. It's considered poor sportsmanship to drop out of a climb when you've only reached the midpoint on a 3,000-foot wall. Conditioning for climbers means vigorous exercise of the legs, back and torso, forearms and upper arms, and hands. Physical therapists recommend working out vigorously four times a week in a well-equipped gym. For strengthening palms and fingers, use squeeze-grippers or squeeze a firm ball. Or milk a cow twice a day. Milking does wonders for the hands. Punching a computer keyboard is meaningless.

KAYAKING AND CANOEING

The strength and condition of the upper-body arm muscles used for paddling are the keys to paddling power as well as dexterity with paddles. Since the upper body is the working machine for both kayaking and canoeing, strengthen it with bench presses, push-ups, and using free weights for exercise.

Edward Craig, an orthopedic surgeon at the Hospital for Special Surgery in New York City, says paddlers can relieve some of the pain of back tension by practicing partial sit-ups and pelvic tilts.

Exercising on a rowing machine is even better.

The 75,000-Mile Guarantee

I'm not talking about your four-by-four but about your feet. I *guarantee* that at about 75,000 miles your feet will start to wear out. Average people reach this milestone at 50; active outdoorspeople can easily reach 75,000 miles at age 40 or even earlier.

The significance of this statistic is that feet lose their natural cushioning as protective fat pads degenerate. Half the natural padding is actually gone at the 75,000-mile mark. The result is that ligaments holding the 26 bones and 33 joints in each foot grow wider and longer. Beyond 75,000 miles, podiatrists say, deterioration seems to accelerate.

A survey in early 1998 by Yankelovich Partners found that nearly half of adult Americans have some type of foot or ankle difficulty, and that for one in five adults, these have required altering or reducing activities.

Dr. Jonathan T. Deland, foot and ankle specialist at the Hospital for Special Surgery, says that in addition to feet simply wearing out, a condition called posterior tibial tendon insufficiency, if untreated, may make walking impossible.

It follows that it's not necessarily a fading spirit of adventure that keeps most over-40s off the trail—but painful foot problems.

It's Not Too Late to Save Your Soles

Here are some of the common foot problems and suggested solutions for those who plan to start hiking the full length of the Pacific Crest Trail on their 80th birthday.

An active outdoorsman, like this park ranger, can easily accrue 75,000 miles of "footwear" by the time he reaches the age of 40.

SHOE SIZE

By age 50, your shoe may be one size larger than it was at 20. For many, this involves the length and width of the forefoot but not the heel. Buy a longer, wider shoe for both trail and normal use. If necessary, use pads on either side of the heel, not a U-shaped insert, to keep the shoe fitting properly.

BUNIONS

These are far more common in women than men because of years of wearing short, narrow shoes. Protect bunions with doughnut-shaped moleskin pads. And begin wearing roomier shoes. Sometimes custom orthotics (inserts) may help in both city shoes and hiking boots.

FALLEN ARCHES

Even those born with fine arches can lose them with age. Loss of arches can result in fatigue or pain in the feet, legs, or lower back. Custom orthotics may bring relief.

MORTON'S NEUROMA

Whether walking in the city or backpacking a wilderness trail, those with this problem may suffer burning, cramping, or severe pain that is relieved only by stopping, taking off their shoes, and massaging the area. Usually all that is necessary to cure the problem is to wear roomier shoes and place protective pads under the involved area. Surgery occasionally is necessary, and is successful in 80 percent of cases.

Have Kids, Will Travel

Whether single or couples, families with children will find unique value in giving youngsters a sense of joy when hiking, biking, canoeing, or camping in the wilderness. Kids can also gain an awareness of the concept of conserving our splendid outdoor resources.

WHEN IS A CHILD FIT FOR WILDERNESS TRAVEL?

Unless car camping in well-used areas, it is generally recommended that infants be at least three months old and examined by the pediatrician before wilderness travel. Parents, of course, are the final judges of the age at

Dad and the kids out for a stroll.

which their child may be involved in outdoor activities, though the tendency among proud Moms and Pops is to overestimate how ready their children are. So here is a summary of recommended minimum ages and fitness guidelines to help you evaluate your own children's readiness.

Canoeing: Under age six, kids are basically guests only. We did meet one couple on a canoe trip in the wilderness of northern Quebec who had been paddling for a week with a year-old baby with them.

Six-year-olds can sit in the bow by themselves and actually do a bit of paddling with short, ultralight plastic paddles. But it really is the parent in the stern who does the work.

Nine-year-olds are ready to paddle bow consistently for fair distances; they're quite capable of handling the stern—with proper instruction—in Class I water. With experience, they can paddle bow or stern in mild (Class I.5) white water. By age 10, active canoeists should have no problems on lengthy canoe trips. However, parents must judge the weight they can carry on portages.

Rafting: Commercial raft organizations recommend a minimum weight of 50 pounds so a child can fit securely in a life jacket; kids also must have the strength to hold on to a rope while the raft is bouncing through serious rapids, and the nature not to panic if something goes wrong.

Mountain Biking: Most nine-year-olds have the skill and strength to handle mountain bikes on relatively easy mountain trails; the child should be at least 4 foot 8 to fit the smallest fat-tire bike frames.

Cross-Country Biking: Eight-year-olds with a multispeed gear bicycle should have no trouble covering 20 miles daily on paved or smooth country roads while totting their share of gear in a pannier and day or backpack.

Backpacking: By age five children can carry their own small packs and have the maturity to "keep moving"; they tend to get excited about little things close at hand, rather than enjoying the sweeping vistas that adults do on the trail.

High-Altitude Backpacking: At 8,000 feet or higher, the generally suggested minimum age is about 10 for moderately strenuous climbs. Above 10,000 feet, both adults and children will acclimate to the altitude far better if they relocate a camp no higher than an additional 1,000 feet each night.

Scuba Diving and Snorkeling: Six. Should be taught both skills only by professionals.

Rock Climbing: Eight to 10 on short, beginner cliffs. Learning, which involves the use of climbing hardware and ropes, is safest on indoor climbing walls under the supervision of climbing experts.

Campground (Car) Camping: No age restrictions.

Winter Camping: Usually kids must be around six before they have the maturity to accept the inconveniences of a snowy winter weekend in a tent.

Snowshoeing: Six; need sturdy leg muscles and dexterity to manipulate lightweight plastic snowshoes.

Cross-Country Skiing: Six; on only a few inches of snow on reasonably level ground.

Alpine Skiing and Snowboarding: Age four with an adult on a gentle trail, or in ski school.

Common sense suggests that children be given frequent breaks on any long-distance activity. Don't feel it necessary to push them beyond a comfortable limit. You're not testing stamina but giving them a sense of the infinite beauty of our sacred wild lands and waters.

Hazy Days

It's not only the humidity that causes hazy days in mountains east of major cities, and much of the Northeast, but pollution from ultraminute particles of sulfate and carbon, and some nitrates suspended in the air. These particles, along with ozone, says Bruce Hill, senior scientist with the Appalachian Mountain Club, work their way deep into the lungs and affect lung function in even the healthiest of hikers. Hill says sulfates come primarily from the combustion of fossil fuels and automobile emissions, especially sport-utility vehicles, trucks, and buses.

2

Getting into Gear, Part I: Boots and Clothing

The day shall not be up so soon as I
To try the fair adventure of tomorrow.
  —*William Shakespeare*
  1564–1616

Choosing the Right Type of Boot

Buying boots for yourself or for the kids? Consider: What type of camping will you be doing? Will you set up a base camp and take occa-

Outdoor shoe soles come in a variety of patterns, all designed to reduce chances of slipping. Smaller patterns inflict the least damage on delicate wilderness turf.

sional trail trips for a day? Serious backpacking? High-elevation mountaineering? Maybe bicycling from campsite to campsite? Canoeing? You will buy better boots for yourself if you recognize the walking you will do in them.

Boots are designed for various uses. *Backpacker* magazine, in a Gear Guide issue, listed these specifications for adult boots:

TECHNICAL SCRAMBLING

These are special lightweight, low-cut shoes for rock climbing.

TRAIL BOOTS

Primarily low or midcut, trail boots are designed for use on well-kept paths when carrying light to moderate loads. They are made in fabric-and-leather combination as well as all-leather models with multiple seams and flexible soles. Check for quality construction, in particular sturdy sewing and good traction.

ROUGH TRAIL BOOTS

Ideal for light backpacking, these boots deliver good support and sole rigidity. The ankle-high uppers should be either leather or a fabric-and-leather combination. Quarter- to half-length steel shanks or semi-stiff plastic midsoles give these boots enough rigidity to handle bumps and lumps.

OFF-TRAIL BOOTS

These are boots that combine support and flexibility. They have heavy-duty soles and high-traction treads. Look for full-grain leather, above-ankle support, rubber rands for abrasion resistance and leak protection, and minimal seams for best waterproofing.

MOUNTAINEERING BOOTS

These are full-grain leather boots that offer ample support for scrambling around on rocks, ice, and snow. They have stiff, aggressive soles with embedded grooves for slipping into crampons. The seamless construction, gusseted tongues, and full-rubber rands minimize leakage. The soles should be rockered for hiking comfort.

DOUBLE BOOTS

These boots have a molded-plastic outer shell and insulated inner boot for warmth. Strictly for winter camping and mountaineering.

Shopping for Boots

After learning all the major points of different shoes, you're still left with a bewildering number of choices in selecting a basic boot. But it's time to go shopping in a store with a wide stock of boots.

FIGURE IT OUT

Expect to pay a minimum of $100 for lighter-weight trail boots, and from $200 to $400 for off-trail and mountaineering boots. What's the cost for kids' boots?

MEASURE UP

Your foot should be measured with a Brannock, a device that measures the length, width,

Note carefully: The triple twist in the middle of the lacing lets you adjust the tightness of the foot area; upper laces are looped over the hooks so they are more secure.

and arch of your foot while you are both sitting down and standing up. After measuring, the salesperson should inspect your bare feet to check for problems, such as calluses or bone spurs, that may require adjustment to your boots by a boot specialist.

GET REAL

When trying on boots, wear the same socks, or combination of socks, that you prefer when on the trail. The boot must feel basically comfortable. Walk around. Up and down steps. If possible, also walk down a steep incline. Do your toes hit the toe of the boot? Try to wiggle your toes. If they don't move easily, you may want to try on a larger size.

TAKE A LAST STAND

Keep in mind that not all boot companies use the same last (design mold). If Brand A just doesn't seem right, try Brand B. This is especially important for women. Many—not all, but many—companies now make a few models specifically for women using a woman's last, rather than merely marking smaller men's boots as women's, as was the custom for many years. (This also is a problem in buying ski boots, where it is equally important for a woman to wear a woman's last and not a small man's boot put into a box marked "Female.")

LIGHTEN YOUR LOAD—NOT YOUR WALLET

Don't be swayed by how many different pieces of Gore-Tex and nylon and plastic and synthetics and leather are cut and sewn to make your boots the coolest. Indeed, a full-grain leather boot with minimum seams, whether low cut or high, will be as fine a boot as you can buy for any level of hiking and backpacking.

However, do be swayed by how much those spanking, sparkling boots weigh and cost. A sturdy pair of expensive above-the-ankle mountain boots can weigh in at over 6 pounds. They may look rough and stylishly mountaineerish. But your legs will end the day a helluva lot happier if they can tramp around in 1½- to 2½-pound boots. And in my experience (despite what salespeople or enticing ads say), lighter boots usually are as serviceable for tough mountain travel, on and off trail, as the giants. And far cheaper. However, far above timberline, when backpacking involves intermittent snows and icy sections, weight may be less important and the height and construction of a heavy boot more significant.

The lighter the boot, the happier your feet will be. One pound can turn into a monstrous difference after backpacking 15 miles.

Moral: When I'm backpacking, I carry a toothbrush with the handle cut off to save weight.

A SHORT COURSE IN ERGONOMICS

Although much is made about how much more ankle support a high boot will give than a low-cut boot, the reality is that there may not be very much, except in the advertisements. In the only study with which I am familiar, rangers in New York's famed Adirondack Mountains found after summarizing foot and ankle injuries that required medical treatment one year that half involved trail hikers wearing low-cut shoes, street shoes, and tennis shoes, and half involved hikers with sturdy ankle-high hiking boots.

The widely used Vibram lug sole with its relatively deep grooves has a reputation for providing excellent protection against slippage. However, some of the new low-impact lug soles offer almost equal stability but are gentler on wet and muddy terrain.

BREAK 'EM IN

An educated guess as to how your new boots will feel on your feet on the trail is to wear them every night for a week at home. Arrange for a money-back guarantee if they simply are not the boots for you.

When you are satisfied you have the right boots, break them in properly—which means at least 20 miles of walking around the house and in the park before you go off for a weeklong trek in the woodlands and over high mountains.

Clothing for Kids
Buy only quality clothing especially designed for outdoor wear, including wool and fleece fibers, but not cottons, just as you wear yourself in camp and climbing a high peak.

Giving Your Kids the Boot

While boots for the young set are made of the same materials as those for adults, boots for kids usually come in three basic styles: a high boot that goes above the ankle, a medium boot that is only ankle high, and a low cut, or below the ankle. Above the ankle are best suited for older, larger children who will be involved in all types of mountain trails both summer and winter. The low or medium are well suited to less vigorous trails and have a distinct advantage over the bigger boots: They do not weigh as much. Low cut, however, pose a problem for those youngsters who can't resist splashing through every puddle on the trail.

Uppers made of full-grain, split-grain, or Nubuk leather are more durable and give better protection than those made of synthetics. However, when wet, the synthetics will dry faster.

In a proper-fitting youngster's boot, the heel will fit somewhat snugly and the toes will have room to wiggle. When the foot is fully in the boot there should be less than ½ inch between the heel and the boot. Test this by putting a finger into the heel of the boot your child is trying on. Also, rub your hands inside the boot to make sure the seams are smooth and not rough.

Buying Used Boots for Kids

It often is possible to buy used hiking boots for children. Some outing goods stores will accept used boots in good condition as partial payment on a new pair, and resell them at a sharp discount below new boots. (This is equally true of children's skis and ski boots.) Also, look for used hiking boots in thrift shops. If you belong to an outdoor organization, you might insert an ad in its local newsletter for boots, or, in turn, offer your child's outgrown boots for sale.

Caring for Your Boots

Keep them clean. If they do not have an inner waterproof lining, such as Gore-Tex, treat them with the water repellent recommended by the manufacturer before outings. When treating boots with goo, be especially careful to rub it into the seams and where the tops fit onto the soles.

These hiking socks may appear fussy, but they're designed logically to give the foot maximum support. When trying on boots, be sure to wear the same socks you wear on the trail.

If the boots get wet, never place them close to a hot fire. Too much heat can burn the thread in the seams, damage leather, or even set synthetic tops on fire. Dry them slowly. This applies particularly to kids warming wet boots in front of a campfire.

Choosing the Right Socks

Wool or the new synthetics are excellent for outdoor wear,

summer or winter, because they will wick away dampness. Cotton socks will not. Some backpackers wear a thin silk or polypropylene liner under wool socks in very cold weather.

Selecting Outdoor Fabrics

To Yvon Chouinard, one of the world's renowned mountaineers, there was only one fabric for the outdoor adventurous.

In his 1978 book, *Climbing Ice,* he wrote: "For breaches, sweaters, shirts, and caps, the answer is wool."

Today, Chouinard's original climbing equipment shop, Patagonia, is one of the nation's largest catalog and outdoor chains servicing the active. Its lines of clothing not only are made of Chouinard's favorite, wool, but also include a variety of clothing made of the material that has transformed the entire garment industry—oil converted into nylon, out of which are manufactured dozens of fabrics, styles, and uses of *fleece*.

FLEECE

Fleece is used in a tremendous range of products: gloves and sweaters, jackets and socks, hats and pants, for inner wear and outer coats. Some fleece is treated to be rain resistant, breathable, and windproof, some has four-way stretch, some feels almost as firm as top-quality wool, some is for campfire warmth, other for sunny days, and some as light and fluffy as a baby's blanket.

What this all adds up to is that whatever you may want in oil converted to nylon and turned into fleece inner and outer clothing—outfits for walking your dog through the park, or wearing at 15,000 feet and climbing, or when backpacking through field and across stream—is available. Go a-lookin'.

WOOL

Mountain veterans for generations have worn wool. It is warm. It wicks water away from the body. It is sturdy. A fine wool

Scout the Internet
Cyberspace has invaded the great outdoors. Before you backpack from store to store in search of everything from boots to tents, you may want to visit *http://www.gearfinder.com.* For general backwoods information, prowl the BaseCamp Encyclopedia: *http://bpbasecamp.com/encyc/.*

pair of pants or shirt, a wool jacket or wool socks will outlast fleece by twice the years. My heavy wool shirt has comforted my chilled bones for more than a quarter century. It still wears as though I bought it only last week. And my tight-weave cuffless wool pants—neither the fabric nor the cuffs will become a gathering place for bugs and weeds—are yet only 20 years old.

I will wear out before they do.

SILK

Silk is what fabric gourmets choose for cold-weather underwear, as a lining for gloves, and as seductive pajamas or nightgowns whether worn in a sleeping bag or between the sheets at home. Like today's polypropylene, silk has been whisking moisture away from the body since the Chinese learned to convert silkworms into fabric 4,000 years ago.

COTTON: THE DEAD MAN'S CLOTHING

For outdoor activity, leave the cotton home. Unless you are beach camping in mild summer weather, cotton is the fabric of last resort. It does not hold in body warmth. When wet, it does not wick the moisture away from your skin. It stays wet. It stays cold. Veteran mountaineers refer to cotton as "Dead Man's Clothing." Let it hang in the closet when you hang out in the wilderness.

SYNTHETICS

Here's a rundown of the most common synthetics for winter and outdoor clothing:

Thinsulate: A polyester blend made by 3M that consists of 35 percent polyester and 65 percent olefin. It's spun into a thin insulation for use in hats, gloves, and outerwear.

Capilene: A polyester fiber from the Patagonia company. It wicks moisture from the skin to the surface, where it evaporates. It's used in underwear, garment linings, and socks.

Thermolite: A Dacron polyester made by DuPont that's used as lightweight insulation in gloves, footwear, and outerwear.

Entrant: An elastic coating of waterproof polyurethane that breathes through microscopic holes that allow body moisture to escape but block rain from penetrating. It's used chiefly in rain gear and to make waterproof gloves.

Polartec: A name for various fabrics made of polyester fleece by Malden Mills. Polartec is made in several weights of polyester pile, a double-sided microfiber, and Lycra stretch.

Synchilla: What Patagonia calls its Polartec filling.

Gore-Tex: The most widely known insulation laminated to outer fabrics. It permits body moisture to escape through microscopic holes that also prevent rain from entering.

Hollofil: A hollow fiber made of Dacron polyester for lower-priced sleeping bags and outer garments. Hollofil II is the premium brand. It resists flattening better than plain Hollofil.

Microloft: A synthetic fiber made of filaments thinner than a human hair. It is used in gloves, outerwear, and sleeping bags.

Microfiber: A fine, tightly woven fiber that breathes while protecting against cold; it's also called, among other names, Super Microft and Versatech.

Polypropylene: Derived from petroleum, this is a strong, paraffin-based fiber that wicks moisture away from the body. It's widely used in underwear and garments next to the skin.

Primaloft: Micropolyester fibers interwoven into a lightweight alternative to down. It's used in sleeping bags and outerwear.

Boots and Clothing Tips

- When buying clothing and gear for your wilderness journeys, buy the best you can afford, whether it is a sleeping bag, hiking socks, or a coil of kernmantle rope. The trail or river is no place to curse a cheap flashlight that doesn't turn on, or a bargain tent whose floor sops up moisture from damp ground.
- As soon as you get married, start saving so you can buy your children the same quality outdoor gear you and your spouse use.
- Polypropylene underwear is a great substitute for Grandma and Grandpa's ancient woolen nightgown.

3

Getting into Gear, Part II: Equipment

We do not go into the green woods and crystal waters to rough it, we go to smooth it. We get it rough enough at home.
  —Nessmuk (George Sears)
    1888

Internal– versus External–Frame Backpacks

Modern backpacks come in two distinct styles, those with an internal frame and those with an external frame.

Internal-frame packs have a frame, usually of graphite or aluminum, built into the pack itself. Both the internal frame and the frame straps can be adjusted to fit an individual's shape. These packs carry a load both lower and closer to the back than the external frame. Although they have padding to protect the back from hard objects, care must be taken to stuff such things as stoves and fuel bottles so they won't dig into you on the trail. The packs are easier to haul around when traveling by car, canoe, or plane than an external-frame pack.

External-frame packs started to go out of fashion in the '80s but now are undergoing a revival. Several factors account for this. One, by way of an example, is that today's models can be adjusted to carry a load at different heights. The highest position puts the pack higher than an

internal-frame pack rides, thus enabling the hiker to stand more upright. The frame also has an air space between the back and the pack itself, which adds considerably to the comfort of carrying a heavy load on a hot day.

Several companies now make internal-frame backpacks especially designed for a woman's anatomy, including the Kelty Tornado, the L. L. Bean Mt. Washington,

The L. L. Bean Mountaineering Pack (left), with a capacity of 5,000 cubic inches for strenuous mountaineering expeditions. Right is a photograph of a companion deluxe Rucksack with half the capacity for long-weekend trips. Courtesy L. L. Bean

and the Osprey Isis. The packs have a shorter length and flared hip belts.

Buying the Right-Sized Pack For You

When shopping for a pack, whether adult or for an eager young hiker, begin with reality. Since this will be a home away from home, it must be able to hold both securely, and as comfortably as possible, *everything* that goes with you on the trail.

If your backpacking will be overnight trips, usually a bag of 2,500- to 3,000-cubic-inch capacity is sufficient. For a week's trek, consider something in the 3,500- to 4,500-cubic-inch range. For longer, and cold-weather trips, begin at 4,500 cubic inches and go to as big a monster as you can carry loaded when climbing a steep pitch on an 8,000-foot mountain.

Next, measure your torso. This, not your overall height, will determine the fit of a pack. Easy enough. Have one of the kids, your spouse, or a friend with friendly hands measure your spine from the seventh vertebra—that's the knob that sticks out from your neck—to the end point, which also is the shelf of your hip bones. A length of 20 inches is a long pack, 18 to 20 is medium long, and under 18, medium. The "torso length" does not materially affect the capacity of the pack you choose.

How Much Weight Should an Adult Carry?

Both outdoor veterans and medical studies on this very subject indicate an adult in good health can carry roughly 20 to 25 percent of body weight. This applies whether the backpacker is a 15-year-old on her first weekend trip with her family, or a sturdy 175-pound man 30 years old. The 20 percent is for the more frail, but that big, powerful lug can carry 30 percent. Or maybe a smidgen more if he wants to help his 115-pound feminine companion lighten her recommended 23-pound load.

Start shopping by loading at least 20 pounds into the backpack of your choice before slipping your arms through the straps. Next check that the hip belt rides on your hips, not on your waist, and that the sternum strap can be adjusted to a comfortable position. Go walking. Upstairs and down. Around the store. Even if the fit is "perfect," it's advisable to try a similar-style pack made by a different company. The comfort level may be even higher.

The clothes you wear will affect the comfort of the pack and pounds you can stuff into your pack. Judge for yourself the difference in the weight and bulk of clothes you don on a cold early-spring trek, and those for backpacking in midsummer.

Backpacks for Kids

It is equally important that children carrying gear and equipment on the trail have a comfortable pack for their age and size. This means they should also go through the same checkout procedures as Mom or Dad before they leave the store. The sensible recourse for the very youngest is a backpack that is, essentially, simply a soft pack without internal or external frames. A good pack will have compression straps that tighten the bag so that small loads will not bounce around, and webbed shoulder straps that run the length of the bag slightly away from the body. Models best suited for light backpacking by children should have padded shoulder straps, back padding, and a padded hip belt.

Sometimes it's the weight of a youngster—not a backpack— that's carried along the trail. This standard kid carrier (left), designed for city streets, lacks the protective sun/rain canopy of the Tough Traveler kid carrier, shown at right.

Remember, a schoolbag is not a backpack, but a backpack can be used to tote books in.

For the older child, both external- and internal-frame pack systems are available. The external-frame packs have one distinct advantage over internal-frame packs: The frames can be adjusted as the child grows. This means that larger packs can be fastened to the same frame for several years. An external-frame system should be usable for the same youngster from about 7 or 8 to 12 years old. By that age, most young outdoor enthusiasts go into adult pack systems.

How Much Weight Should a Child Carry?

Dr. John Kella, a consultant who advises companies on ergonomics, says youngsters less than 10 years old should "try not to carry more than 10 to 15 percent of their body weight" to avoid strain on shoulders, neck, and upper back. Dr. Bernard A. Rawlins, a spine specialist at the Hospital for Special Surgery, says that a pack should always be worn with both arms through the shoulder straps because they distribute the weight evenly.

As with all expensive items, do make certain you can return a pack if, after its new owner, adult or youngster, carries heavy loads around the house in it for a week, it does not fit comfortably.

How Much Weight Should a Dog Carry?

Veterinarians say the load carried by your canine buddy in his pannier can range from 15 to 25 percent of his body weight.

Waterproofing Your Backpack

To ensure that a new pack is reasonably waterproof, seal all the seams with tent seam sealer. I also spray my well-used pack with a water repellent, Silicone Water-Guard, once a year. However, the manufacturer of a pack may recommend a different water-resistant spray. You understand, naturally, that in a storm water still manages to creep in. Thus, everything that must be protected against moisture should be stuffed into tough plastic garbage bags before being shoved into the pack. Stuff in a couple of extra plastic bags along with everything else.

Remember, the Gordon Bag System (see chapter 4) is as effective for keeping track of gear on a group backpacking trek as it is on a canoe adventure or when car or bicycle camping. Use it to divide food and equipment among all the backpackers according to their individual ability to carry weight.

Put Your Backpack Through the Paces

For an easy start on any type of cross-country travel, take a first-timer for a one-day trip, with a stop for lunch, while carrying the weight in the pack that he or she will tote on a wilderness trek. A long stretch of some 10,000 miles of abandoned railroad track throughout the United States converted to recreational use could be ideal. To locate any in your area, contact the Rails-to-Trails Conservancy.

How Much Do Backpacks Cost?

For acceptable-quality trail backpacks, expect to pay from $150 to $200 for the smaller, lighter packs to a high of between $400 and $500 for the tough, rugged big boys.

Personal Canoe Bags: The Canoeist's "Backpack"

While trail backpacks may certainly be used by paddlers, and frequently are, it's a more sensible option to buy a "backpack" specifically for canoeists.

Trudging off to his canoe, a paddler has all personal gear stuffed in a totally waterproof bag that is worn like a backpack on the portage trail.

These are large, "vertical" waterproof bags with shoulder straps that can be carried on your back along a portage or through an airport.

The top-quality bags are made of tough PVC-coated fabric and a reinforced bottom. They are made with a roll-down top that can be cinched to keep even a hint of water from seeping in, and thick, padded, adjustable shoulder straps.

A bag with a 2-cubic-foot capacity generally is fine for the personal gear for one person; two paddlers can share a 4-cubic-footer.

Dry bags need special care, though, when carrying sharp objects. Pack them in the center. Solvents can damage vinyl. If any spills on your bag, wash it off promptly. Occasionally wipe a dry bag with 303 Protectant to keep the vinyl supple.

Bagging a Good Night's Sleep

A fine sleeping bag is not the only ingredient necessary for a night of comfort and cloudless dreams, whether you're tucked inside a tent or sleeping under the stars. But it's damned important.

Finding the right bag for your comfort and pocketbook will not be accomplished by darting into an outing store, no matter how well equipped, and grabbing the first one the sales clerk recommends. Before that happens, do some basic homework. What kind of camping do you usually do? Only pleasant summers at the beach? Backpacking summer and winter? Traveling via canoe or bike? Carrying all the gear in the car to where you set up camp? Once you determine your outdoor style, you're on the trail of bagging a good night's sleep.

MINIMUM COMFORT RATINGS

With your outdoor style in mind, consider then the "minimum comfort rating" that manufacturers set for their various bags—though the ratings are more an educated guess than a fact, and cannot take into account whether you sleep warm while your partner is shivering.

Now look at these factors: For the high-mountain backpacker or winter cross-country skier, consider a comfort rating of no less than 10 to –10 degrees F. For the three-season camper, look for a rating of between 20 and 30 degrees F. For the summer only, a minimum of 40 degrees F. Then add that you are quite willing to either don long johns and wool socks when the temperature plummets, or refuse to put on anything but the radio when you climb into the bag in warm weather.

FILL POWER MAKES THE DIFFERENCE

The most important element in the warmth-weight ratio is the filling. No synthetic has yet been developed that can expand larger and compress smaller, pound for pound, than upper-quality down. The quality of down has nothing to do with whether it comes from a duck waddling around in China or a northern goose. What is significant—let me repeat, what is significant—is the "fill power" of the down: that is, how many cubic inches an ounce of down will fill.

Minimum-quality good down has a fill power of 550. In other words, an ounce of down will expand to fill 550 cubic inches. Top-quality fill power ranges from 700 up. *If the label on a down bag does not specify the fill power, no matter how famous the outlet that sells it, or that the bag is filled with "prime down"—a meaningless phrase—hang it back on the rack.*

Today, bags filled with excellent synthetic materials are far more popular than down bags. The chief reason: price. The chief drawbacks: weight and bulk. For bags of roughly equal minimum comfort, a synthetic bag will weigh 25 to 40 percent more than a down bag. Among the top synthetics, Quallofil, Hollofil II, and Polargard 3D are slightly heavier than LiteLoft, Primaloft, or Polargard High Void for the same fill power, though the latter three do not stand up quite as well.

SLEEPING BAG STYLES

Sleeping bags come in three basic styles: mummy, semimummy, and rectangular. A good mummy or semimummy will have a boxed foot section to keep your feet warm, because the shape helps the filling retain its loft. To sleep cuddled up with your partner, consider matched bags that can be zipped together.

Women now have the option of buying sleeping bags that take into consideration the difference in physical shape between them and a male body. Female gender designs are offered by The North Face, Eastern Mountain Sports, and Lafuma America.

When it comes to sleeping bags for kids—don't skimp! They need to keep warm at night, too.

A top-quality, mummy-style sleeping bag will be slightly roomier at the bottom for wiggling feet. For year-round use, the bag should also have a hood to cover the head when the thermometer plunges.

HOW MUCH DO SLEEPING BAGS COST?

At this time, quality synthetic bags range roughly from $90 to $150. Top-quality down bags range from $200 to $500 plus. Keep in mind that some outing stores accept used children's bags for a partial discount on buying larger bags.

THE FINAL ANALYSIS

Finally, before buying a sleeping bag, study the annual equipment guides published by outdoor magazines. Look at their evaluation of down and manufactured fill materials, the weight of the bag, comfort rating, and quality. And such items as a zipper that is protected with an overflap, or whether the bag has a built-in hood. And follow either the advice of the Mayan sage who said: "An ounce on your back is a pound on the trail"—or that of the wise, old Inuit medicine man who noted: "Sleeping bag like blubber on seal. Skinny seal always cold."

AVOIDING WET BAGS

Makers of synthetic bags proudly point out that if the sleeping bag gets wet, it can be wrung out and still retain its loft. Down, when wet, shrivels into a big, wet facecloth. To some, this is reason enough not to

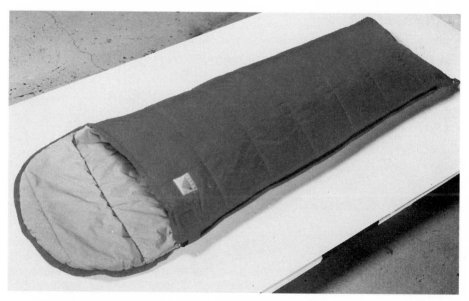

A rectangular bag is not as confining as the mummy, but is not as warm for sleeping, unless, of course, two identical rectangular bags . . .

take a down bag canoeing, or even backpacking when stormy weather threatens. Nonsense. Carry a sleeping bag in a waterproof stuff sack. Treat it carefully. In more than a few decades of canoeing only with down-filled bags, I've had nary a problem.

By the way: Never buy a sleeping bag with sewn-through seams, unless it's for the children sleeping in a backyard tent.

DON'T GET STUCK BETWEEN A ROCK AND A HARD PLACE

The ground is hard. The ground is cold. And your expensive sleeping bag compresses as thin underneath you as a sheet. So get yourself a sleeping pad.

The only type to avoid are the old-fashioned air bags. They float. They keep your butt off the ground. But each time you breathe, the air inside the bag circulates and the bit of warmth next to your body is replaced by a cold draft from air next to the ground.

There are, basically, three types of sleeping pads: closed-cell foam, open-cell foam, and foam-filled self-inflating pads.

The closed cell, popular with backpackers, are fine for keeping out the cold, but since they generally range in thickness from ¼ to ½ inch, they are solid, uncomfortable, and do little to keep rocks and roots from digging into you all night.

Camper-style open-cell pads usually range in thickness from 1 to 2 inches. They are comfortable. They do keep you off the chilly ground. But they are bulky and awkward to carry.

. . . are zipped together for a couple.

Self-inflating sleeping pads—such as the Therm-A-Rest—range from about 1 to 1½ inches thick when open for a night's snooze. They can be rolled virtually as tight as a closed-cell pad. These bags contain a filling that expands when the bag is open. The filling keeps the air in the bag from circulating.

Try lying on the three types of sleeping pads on the floor of the outing goods store on your next "gottahavit" expedition before you toss them onto your credit card.

HOW TO CARE FOR AND CLEAN YOUR SLEEPING BAG

Keep pads and sleeping bags clean. A down-filled bag should never be dry-cleaned except by cleaners who use *only* the special solution that will not harm down. It is so flammable, however, that most cities do not permit its use. Wash a bag only with pure soap, or the solution sold for washing down, in warm or cool water. If possible, use a front-loading washer with a rotating drum, not a top-loading home washer with a circulating spiral, which may damage the bag.

Dry at a minimum temperature. Do not toss a tennis shoe into the dryer with your bag. Not necessary. Let the dryer do all the work.

For washing synthetics, follow the manufacturer's directions.

When camping, air out your sleeping bag every morning.

When not on the trail or in camp, store all bags, synthetic or down, in a large, loose bag.

Color Your World

Some low-impact extremists frown at tents, sleeping bags, or bags in which to store gear or food in any color but a dull, non–visually impacting gray, green, or camouflage. With children in the wilderness, nonsense! Buy a child's bag in a bright color that's easily seen when it is forgotten hanging on an outstretched branch in the morning after everyone is packed and ready to hit the trail. A red or yellow tent is far easier to spot in the distance than one of subdued color. Whether you're packing them in the car or loading them into the canoes, food and utility bags are easy to spot if their bright colors shout, "Hey, here I am, stupid!"

Indian Tepees

Tepees, also known as wickiups, wigwams, and hogans, were the dwellings used by American Indians. The nomadic Plains tribes made theirs of buffalo hides stretched around a cone of poles perhaps 10 to 12 feet high. They were strong, waterproof, and easy to move. It is not unusual today to see an occasional tepee made of sheets of canvas instead of hides on Indian reservations.

Southern and western tribes originally made their tepees of mats or brush laid over arched poles. It is possible today to stay in an authentic Navajo "hogan," as they called their dwellings, when traveling across the Navajo reservation. The Navajo coated their hogans with clay. B&Bs are offered by Navajo women. Breakfast is cooked on a small wood-stove inside the hogan, rather than over the traditional open fire.

Tents Old and New

As infantry draftees in World War II, we carried canvas shelter halves—small tarps about 6 feet by 8 feet. When two were buttoned together, they made a floorless two-person tent that buttoned at both ends. When it rained, if you accidentally bumped the tent, where you rubbed against it the water dripped through.

On a recent canoeing trip in late September on the headwaters of the Ottawa River in northwestern Canada, I relaxed inside the tent I carry today. It's a self-supporting four-season two- to three-person dome-style Moss tent with front and rear doors with no-see-um webbing. The fly that almost completely covers the tent extends well beyond the back door, providing a closed vestibule for storing equipment outside the usable tent space. The floor is made of fully waterproof material. You can sleep against the wall and it will not leak in the heaviest rain.

My, how times have changed.

SHOP THE GREAT OUTDOORS

Before you shop for your first tent, check 'em out. Not at the outing goods stores. Start by driving to a few campsites and examining the wide variety of tents campers erect, from single person to huge tents large enough for a family of eight. Be friendly. Ask questions: Is this model hard to put up? What's it like in a real storm? How many people sleep in it? Do you know what it weighs? Does the flooring get wet in rain?

Next, read about tents in the annual equipment issues of outing magazines, especially *Backpacker* and *Outside*.

SHOPPING AT THE OUTING GOODS STORE

Now, go shopping indoors. When you finally spot the tent of probable choice, crawl inside with sleeping bag and gear. Lie down. Get up. Would you be comfortable in it at night? Could you spend hours here sitting out a wild storm? Do you really believe it will meet your future needs? Can you afford it?

HOW MUCH DO TENTS COST?

Summer or three-season two- or three-person tents will sell for around $100 to $200; top-quality four-season two- or three-person tents range from $500 to $1,000.

Everything fit together? Buy it.

THE BACKYARD TEST

No spanking-new tent ever goes a-camping without a backyard checkout. Put it up. A self-supporting tent sometimes takes a

The Family-Sized Tent

Large family tents with a couple of "rooms" are less than ideal for camping. First, there is always confusion with the kids around underfoot. Second, family tents are huge affairs, easily weighing 30 to 40 pounds, difficult to erect, and rarely set up more than a few feet from the car.

Far better: a separate tent for children age three and older. Two lightweight tents can easily be carried on short backpacking trips. Important: A tent for the kids should be the same quality as the one their parents use.

This family, tent-camping its way across the country, carries two tents: one for the kids, one for the parents. Tent sites are widely available at state and national parks and forests, as well as commercial campgrounds.

few tries to get all the wands in properly. Then put the fly on backward. On low- and moderately-priced tents, reseal all seams on the fly and on the floor. When the seams are thoroughly dry, replace the fly, haul out the hose, and see how well the tent sheds rain.

HOW TO CARE FOR AND PROTECT YOUR TENT

It's as true today as it was when first uttered by a Sumerian general in the quartermaster corps: "Archers and spear bearers. I remind you. Take care of your tent and it will take care of you."

When you pitch your tent, pitch it on a plastic drop cloth slightly smaller than the dimensions of the tent. This will protect the tent floor from rocks and roots as well as provide a barrier to keep the tent floor dry if the ground is damp or wet.

UV light rays eventually will cause the fly fabric to deteriorate. When you have a choice, pitch your tent in the shade of trees.

Here's the ideal way to decide on your next tent. If it's a two-person tent, future occupants—with their sleeping bags—should crawl in and check out the comfort factor while the tent still stands in the outing goods tent department.

In camp or on the trail, when taking your tent down, brush it out, shake it off, and dry it before putting it away. *Note to backpackers:* A thoroughly dry tent is noticeably lighter than a damp one.

Never store a tent wet. That's an invitation for mold and mildew. To eliminate the moldy odor from a well-used tent, spray it with the odor eliminator sold at almost every outing goods store.

STUFFING TENTS

Generations of campers have historically been taught to neatly fold a tent, then put it in a stuff bag. No longer. Even tent manufacturers agree that folding a tent the same way time after time may weaken seams and fabric on the folds. Today we stuff 'em. Just like a sleeping bag.

YOU NEED A BIGGER TENT BAG

One of the lessons novice wilderness travelers quickly pick up is that the bag the intriguing new self-supporting tent came in is the wrong size.

In the outing goods store, the factory-packed tent and the necessary poles and pegs neatly and tightly fit inside the bag the clerk hands you.

Beautiful.

Your first weekend trip teaches you something. Once it is unrolled and set up, the tent begins to expand. Slightly. The wind ruffles the fabric. The dirt has to be swept away. Now, especially if it is raining, try, try with muscle, sweat, and grim grit, and eventually you will get the wet tent, and poles, and possibly even some tent pegs into the new, gleaming tent bag.

Avoid the pain, the hostility.

The day you buy that tent, buy a slightly larger waterproof bag to stuff it in.

INCREASE YOUR LIVING SPACE WITH A TARP

Unless you are a lean, mean, high-altitude backpacker, take a tarp on your outings. Sudden rain? Up goes the tarp over the work area and table. Blistering sun? The tarp makes excellent shade. The camping family with separate tents for themselves and the kids will find the tarp

Don't Trip

We all know the awkward feeling of tripping over a tent or tarp cord at night when all we're trying to do is find the john without flashing a light to wake the others. Solution: Make anti-tripping devices known as TPs. Simple. Tie bows of toilet paper on the treacherous ropes. They can be instantly spotted at night.

makes a welcome open-air family room. After the tarp is up, pitch tents so just their front doors are under the tarp.

I carry a 10-by-10 tarp of long staple Egyptian cotton. It sheds rain. It weighs less than 2 pounds. It is strong.

The 3-ounce-per-square-yard reinforced high-count taffeta nylon coated with waterproof urethane makes an excellent tarp or ground cloth. A 10-by-10 will weigh about 2 pounds.

There are really only two effective ways to erect an overhead tarp when you don't carry four corner poles and a center pole. The first is to sling it over a tight rope, strung between two trees, as a ridge pole, with the four corners held by cords pegged to the ground, or tied to trees. The second is to tie the four corners to trees and push up the center with a pole. Before the era of sensitive camping, we would chop down a tall sapling and trim it for a center pole. Today, we carry an adjustable aluminum center pole. At this writing, an adjustable 8-foot pole can be ordered for about $8 from Texsport, 1332 Conrad Sauer, Houston, TX, 77043.

Wroooong. Lacking a high center point, or ridgeline, this tarp will collect a few barrels of water with a couple of minutes of heavy rain. Look out below.

The Hiking Staff—Your Best Friend

On the trail, your most valuable accessory is—the hiking staff. Whether you make your own or buy an adjustable hiking stick at an outing store, put one into your hand before you start. If you have never used one, you will discover swiftly how valuable it is in helping you adjust your balance on difficult stretches, crossing a log across a stream, saving you from a bad fall on a steep drop in the trail, or serving as a "third leg" on an easy trail. Using one or even two staffs will take stress off knees and ankles—especially important for older hikers.

I chopped mine from a grove of hemlock trees many years ago. It has two short branches, each about 2 inches long. One is where I hold it while walking. This is at a point where my "hiking" arm is parallel to the ground from elbow to wrist. However, the staff is some 10 inches longer, with a second branch near the top.

It is quite amazing how handy that

Each notch on my hiking stick represents a hike of 50 miles or longer along various segments of the Appalachian Trail.

upper branch is. I can reach far out and pull a branch toward me, especially if there are a few apples growing on it. Or reach down and drag something out of the water. Using a sharp knife, I have engraved into my hiking staffs the number of miles each has covered when they were my ever-dependable third arm on the trail.

Occasionally I rub my staff down with oil before putting it in a basement corner next to my backpacks awaiting my next trail trek. I have fitted the bottom of the staff with a large rubber cap, such as those used on chair and furniture legs. It helps keep the staff from slipping.

Commercial adjustable staffs have an advantage over mine. They can be compressed and stuffed inside a pack when traveling.

Rope—A Lifeline in the Wilderness

Not only can a coil of rope be a most useful item to toss into your pack, but most outdoor veterans consider it essential. It makes no difference what kind of camping you will be doing—backpacking, bicycling, canoeing, or car camping—and it's immaterial whether you hie off in hot summer or when the winds moan as you snowshoe to your site.

In other words, take rope.

Consider just a few of the important and pleasant things you can do with a rope: Use it for a clothesline, to hang gear on, to rescue a canoeist splashing in a white-water upset, to haul something up a cliff, or to rappel yourself down. As a ridge pole for a tarp tent. Or simply to practice tying knots (see chapter 11).

You will use it.

But only if you have it.

TYPES AND CARE OF ROPES

The usual ropes that most campers carry are made of natural fibers, such as sisal, manila, and cotton. However ropes far superior in breaking strength for their size are made today basically out of nylon under such trade names as polypropylene, Dacron, and Peron.

Synthetic ropes come in two styles: One is the classic twisted construction, where three or four strands are twined around each other. The second is kernmantle. This is made of long inner filaments covered with a woven outer sheath.

Twisted   Kernmantle

Kernmantle is the choice of 99.9 percent of rock climbers, and is increasingly used by traditional campers. If you don't see coils of kernmantle hanging in the local hardware store, visit the nearest camping store.

Fabric ropes are kept from coming apart at the ends either by weaving an inch or two of the end strands back into the rope, or by wrapping them with tape—which, naturally, eventually pulls off.

To keep synthetic rope from coming apart, use a match. Light the end, let it flare briefly, then wipe burning strands with a heavy cloth. This will pull the tip into a ravelproof thin strand instead of leaving a thick glob larger than the diameter of your rope.

All ropes last longer, whether used only as a line to hang gear on in camp or for rock climbing, if handled with sensible care. Eastern Mountain Sports gives its customer this advice on handling synthetic climbing rope (it is equally valid for *all* rope):

Protect it from acids, alkalines, oxidizing agents and bleaching compounds. Gasoline and oil don't cause any appreciable damage but they do attract dirt which can shorten a rope's life. Wash dirty ropes in cold water with a mild, nondetergent soap. Fabric softeners improve (synthetic) rope flexibility by relubricating the fibers. Do not use bleach. Store rope out of the sun. Transport your rope in its own protective bag.

In other words, when you pack your gear in a car before heading off into the wilderness, don't throw the rope in the tool kit.

Frequently used rope that may become critical in an emergency situation should be replaced every year or two. Damaged rope should be replaced before your next outing.

THE BEST ROPE FOR YOU

You must be your own judge based upon the type of activity you enjoy and expect to use it for. If you are a canoeist, one of the critical ropes to have is a floating rescue rope, a 3/8-inch polypropylene rope from 50 to 75 feet long, stored in a "throw" bag. Water rescue ropes are not intended for general use around camp.

I recommend that backpackers, mountain trail bikers, car campers, and canoeists carry 25 to 50 feet of rope for general camp use. Regardless of whether they use a fabric or kernmantle rope, it should have a breaking strength of no less than 2,500 pounds if it might be put into service in an emergency. If the salesclerk cannot verify the breaking strength, promptly hike elsewhere.

My suggestion for general-use rope is kernmantle. It comes in two basic styles, dynamic and static. The dynamic is designed to stretch when subject to a sudden impact; the static is a bit firmer and does not stretch. Rope labeled "dry" is treated with a water-repellent coating. It will float.

Before you buy a rope, hold it in your hands. Feel the grip you can  apply to it. Anything less than 3/8 inch, 9 mm, is apt to be too small to hold securely in your hands for emergency use, though fine for every other job you can put it to. The 7/16 inch, or 11 mm—the size favored by rock climbers—is an excellent rope for all campers and hikers, pedalers and paddlers.

Popular sizes of kernmantle rope range from 7 to 11 mm.

LINK UP WITH CARABINERS

Carabiners, often called snap links, are essential for rock climbers. All of them are sort of oval or D shaped, differing chiefly in whether they simply snap shut or are screwed shut, and in their holding strength. They also can be of exceptional value to the rest of the outdoor fraternity. Backpackers, campers, and canoeists can use them as static pulleys for everything from holding up the center of a tarp on a ridge-pole rope to hauling an 80-pound clunker of a canoe up a steep slope.

Here, by way of an example, is how to double your pulling power when hauling that canoe to the top of the slope. But only if you have both rope and snap link:

Step one: Tie one end of the rope to a tree or rock at the top of the slope.

Step two: Fasten a carabiner to the bow of the canoe.

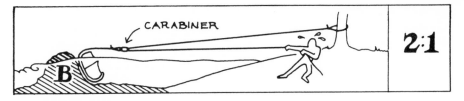

CARABINER

2:1

Carabiners can double your pulling power.

Step three: Put the loose end of the rope through the carabiner and bring it back to the tree.

Step four: Pull. Your pulling power is doubled.

Step five: Whey didn't you think of that before?

Considering what value they may be on your next wilderness trip, visit the outing goods store that handles ropes and gear for climbers. Pick out a couple to snap onto your belt.

PFDs—A Paddler's First Defense

They are known variously as life jackets and lifesavers, but to the Coast Guard they are PFDs, or Personal Flotation Devices. They come in five styles:

Type I are big, bulky affairs worn chiefly by sailors.

Type II are shaped sort of like a horse collar with the bulk of the material across the chest so they will float an unconscious person face-up. Popular with liveries.

Type III look much like a down vest made from foam panels or Ensolite tubes. They are popular with most paddlers.

Type IV are either boat cushions or doughnut rings at swimming pools. Not recommended for paddlers.

Type V are various hybrids ranging from a sort of Type I popular with white-water raft operators to flotation belts for water-skiers.

They come in sizes for adults and children. Children and nonswimmers should

PFD Advisory

No one rafting, canoeing, or kayaking should ever step into a waterborne vehicle without a PFD. Must it be worn at all times? Not necessarily; you can go without when paddling quiet streams or lakes without a wind. But if it's not on your back, it must be in plain sight where it can be donned instantly if the water or weather changes. *Remember: PFDs should never be used as seat cushions, not even by the stupid.*

only wear a PFD with the most flotation material in the front to hold the face up, and, for the littlest, with crotch straps so they don't slip over the head in case of an unexpected splash.

Only buy PFDs that specifically note they meet Coast Guard specifications.

Equipment Tips

- Carry the directions that came with your spanking-new tent on which poles go where the first time you head into the wilds with it.
- Expensive equipment won't make you a better camper, hiker, or canoeist. Your attitude and experience will.
- Halogen flashlight bulbs will burn out batteries three times faster than regular bulbs.
- Carry spare batteries for any power equipment, from watch to flashlight to camera, before heading for a wilderness trip in another country.
- Tents do become damp simply from breathing and moisture from the human body. So? So always hang your tent up when you get home to thoroughly dry it and it won't become smelly from mildew.
- A small role of duct tape can be a hiker or canoeist's wilderness friend when canoes or equipment or even clothes need a patching hand. Carry one with you. You'll find a good use for it, just as I did on a trip when I mended a long tear in my pants suffered while scrambling over a barbed-wire fence.
- Larger sporting goods stores generally rent almost any camping equipment you don't have for a wilderness outing, whether it's a fine tent, a camp stove, a sleeping bag, or snowshoes.
- Sleeping under a cheap, lightweight tarp open to the healthy air instead of a tent sounds like a fine idea—until squadrons of blood-thirsty mosquitoes dive-bomb you awake at four o'clock in the morning.
- Lightweight fleece VBLs, or vapor barrier liners, commonly sold at outing goods stores for keeping a bag clean, will also make your bag slightly warmer.

4

Packing for a Wilderness Outing

A book of verses underneath the bough,
A jug of wine, a loaf of bread and thou
Beside me singing in the wilderness,
Oh wilderness were paradise enow.
  —Omar Khayyám
    1048–1122

Planning Makes Perfect

The most significant element in planning an outdoor trip is not the anxious desire to shed city life for the wilderness but organizing the elements of that great outing before you start packing the car. It will save

many an argument, much confusion in camp, and lots of hidden items that don't emerge until the next day if you arrange your food, equipment, and gear on a planned basis.

The Gordon Bag System

This is an excellent system for keeping food supplies, kitchen material, and general

The Gordon Bag System at work.

camp items organized, whether your outing is with the family or a large group. It consists of three "utility" bags, each well marked on the outside, plus the bags for food.

THE FOOD UTILITY BAG

This contains all of the items that come out at every meal, such as a variety of herbs and spices, salt, sugar, coffee, tea, hot chocolate, powdered juices, extra flour, and plastic bottles of vinegar, lemon juice, olive oil, and cooking wine. Keeping the food utility bag well stocked saves the time-consuming job of putting daily items for each individual meal in each day's food bag.

THE KITCHEN UTILITY BAG

This contains all of the pots, pans, kitchen utensils, and other items necessary for your camp kitchen. It also can include cups, plates, and tableware, or these can be carried by individuals. To keep everything in quick-find order, use individual bags for nesting pots, utensils, and such. Pots and pans used over fire will blacken on the outside. Don't clean them off; blackened pots absorb heat. Use leaves to separate the nesting pots. Stuff them into their own inner bag. Put your bar of laundry soap, no detergents, and a sturdy pot cleaner with the nesting pots.

THE CAMP UTILITY BAG

This is your camping drawer. In it go such items for your particular trip as a portable saw or small hatchet with a file; extra kernmantle rope, 50 feet of strong cord, carabiners, tent pegs, seam sealer, duct tape, portable stove and fuel, a bag with small pliers and Phillips-head and regular screwdrivers, plus some nails; extra poncho, camp tarp, camp lantern, waterproof matches, canoe rescue throw bag when in camp, 3 feet of $\frac{1}{4}$-inch rubber tubing for a mouth bellow, miniature oil can, sewing kit, and grill.

For large groups, the most practical utility bags are horizontal, with shoulder straps.

Who's On Duty?

There is no necessity for anything serious in arranging work schedules for a family, or when traveling with a couple of friends. The larger the group, however, the more important it becomes to work out a formal duty roster so everyone shares all the jobs, and no one finds it convenient to be served without serving. I set up four basic jobs, each handled by a team of two. Job assignments begin at dawn and rotate daily. They are:

COOKS:	They do all the cooking.
FIRE/WATER:	They fill camp pots before each meal; build necessary fires; gather firewood.
BULL COOKS:	A North Woods term for the KPs who do *all* the cleaning of both personal and community kitchen equipment.
SAFETY/CLEAN UP:	They ensure that no unsafe practices occur in camp or underway; responsible for cleaning up garbage and carrying a garbage sack with them, and that each campsite is cleaner when we leave than when we arrived.

The duty roster is worked out before we head off. On canoe trips, no two work together who paddle together. Hey, they've already had a whole day to themselves.

DUTY ROSTER

JOBS	MONDAY	TUESDAY	WEDNESDAY	THURSDAY
COOKS	Pat/Jean	Kevin/Paula	Gail/Bob	Jim/Rell
FIRE/WATER	Kevin/Paula	Gail/Bob	Jim/Rell	Pat/Jean
BULL COOKS	Gail/Bob	Jim/Rell	Pat/Jean	Kevin/Paula
SAFETY	Jim/Rell	Pat/Jean	Kevin/Paula	Gail/Bob
OFF	(if there are more than eight)			

Planning Meals

Enjoy what you eat in the wilderness. Select and cook as a campfire gourmet. Backpackers, of course, must compromise between the weight on their backs and the quality of the meals in their bowls. Casting off ounces is the winner. This is also a consideration for bicycle campers. Canoeists have less of a problem with weight, even when their trip involves an occasional scramble ashore to portage around a set of mean rapids. As for car campers, their chief necessity is a trunk large enough to carry all the delicious goodies they wish to gorge on.

In planning food, it's helpful to work out a master menu for each day, then list each item for each meal, and break that into actual amounts of what will be purchased at the supermarket. The amounts must be based upon the caloric needs per person. The food charts in chapter 9 are a quick way to estimate food values.

After all the food is purchased, next comes the packing. All liquids go only into plastic bottles. Useless packaging is tossed into the recycling bins at home. Remember: When throwing out the package, save the directions.

Finally, each day's food, with a copy of the menu and recipes, is packed in its own bag with a plastic inner bag for waterproofing, if necessary. Then each individual bag is marked on the outside with DAY and NUMBER—for example, MONDAY, DAY ONE; TUESDAY, DAY TWO; and so on.

Some outdoor veterans will use a slightly different system, marking bags by contents, such as BREAKFASTS; LUNCHES; DINNERS.

Are Freeze-Dried Foods for You?

An outing on-your-back inevitably involves freeze-dried and dehydrated foods to minimize weight. I do use them—but only for individual vegetables, starches, and meats. I find two specific problems with the wild plethora of precooked and freeze-dried or dehydrated dishes attractively packaged on every outing store's shelves. First, the manufacturer overestimates, usually by double, the number of people each will serve. The reality is in the caloric content listed on the package. Second, the foods tend to be pitifully lacking in flavor. To compensate, try adding a dash of lemon juice, vinegar, wine, or spices from your food utility bag.

Personal Gear: A Suggested Packing List

This is a recommended—not mandatory—list of personal and community gear to consider for your outdoor adventure, whether car camping, afoot, afloat, or bicycling.

1. Unless you are car camping and have unlimited trunk space, pack light.

    Backpackers should limit total weight, including food, to 20 to 25 percent of body weight until they've had enough experience to determine how much they can carry. A sturdy dog can carry 20 to 25 percent of her body weight, including pannier.

    The only time canoeists need to worry about the weight of a pack is on a portage. However, a canoe should always show at least 6 inches above the water level when fully loaded.

2. Basic clothing: Pants, wool or polyester, tight weave without cuffs; sturdy shirts with long sleeves to protect arms from hungry mosquitoes; polypropylene underwear. Shorts for warm weather. Cotton is *not* recommended in mountain travel.

It's more comfortable to carry a head flashlight with a battery pack that hangs around your neck than the widely used lights with the batteries inside the light container itself. In this model by Petzl, the pack contains an extra set of fresh batteries.

3. Vest-jacket: A fleece or down vest plus wind- and rain-resistant jacket.

4. Rain gear: For backpackers, a poncho that can protect you and cover your pack in rain, plus light nylon rain pants—seams coated with seam sealer—long enough to cover ankles. For paddlers, rain suit only. Feet can get tangled in a poncho. Ponchos are handy for covering gear in a canoe or in camp.

5. Boots: For backpackers, lightweight, low-cut or ankle-high boots are recommended for general trail travel; sturdier boots for winter or high-mountain climbing. Treat per manufacturer's directions for waterproofing. For paddlers, old tennis shoes, river sandals, or wet-suit booties when canoeing; light hiking boots for camp.

Are Ya Dry?

Waterproof test: Load pack. Put on rain gear and pack. Step into bathtub. Turn on shower for 10 minutes. Step out. Remove gear from pack. Everything dry? Are you?

Levis or jeans. In style, but forget them. They are made of cotton.

6. Sunglasses with full UVA plus UVB protection. For long days in bright sun, wraparound or glacier style.
7. Hat. Wide brimmed, water resistant.
8. Socks. Wool or polypro, with padded soles.
9. No expensive jewelry, watches, or the like.
10. Tableware: Cup, multiuse large bowl, fork, spoon, *sharp* sheath or pocket-knife, blade not over 3 inches long.
11. Insect repellent.
12. Toilet paper, one roll per person per week.
13. Unless winter camping, a three-season tent is fine.
14. Toilet kit with small towel.
15. Sunscreen and moisturizer. Apply daily.
16. Sleeping bag.
17. Sleeping pad—air mattress not recommended.
18. Plastic bottle or canteen for water.
19. Matches in waterproof package.
20. Plastic bags. For backpackers, all gear should be stuffed in plastic bags to protect against rain and water. Paddlers should carry gear in fully waterproof bags with shoulder straps for carrying on portages.
21. On the trail carry moleskin for foot problems, and antiperspirant to apply daily to feet.
22. Hiking staff.
23. Gloves.
24. Small musical instrument, optional.
25. Camera, field glasses, optional.
26. Small flashlight with fresh batteries.
27. Spare flashlight batteries and spare bulb.
28. Light shoes for in-camp wear, optional.
29. Candle in candle lantern, optional.
30. Something to read, optional.
31. Water purification tablets.

32. For cold nights, cap to keep exposed head warm.
33. Personal medication.
34. Extra pair of glasses.
35. Whistle—one for every person, young or old.

And _____

_____

_____

Community Gear: A Suggested Packing List

1. 50 feet of light (9 to 11 mm) dry kern-mantle rope.
2. Two carabiners (see page 40).
3. Small *sharp* hatchet, or small fold-up camp saw.
4. Minimum number of pots, pans, and cooking equipment. Select carefully. Largest pot should hold 1 quart water for each person.
5. Backpacking stove with extra fuel.
6. Grill if campfire cooking.
7. First-aid kit.
8. Compass and topographical map.
9. Large safety pins and needle-and-thread kit.
10. Knife sharpener.
11. Collapsible water bucket.
12. Emergency throw rope for canoeists.
13. Light tarp, optional. Only not optional when it rains.

And _____

_____

_____

Let There Be Light

High-intensity flashlight bulbs are a severe shock to the length of service you will get out of batteries. High-power alkaline batteries are a luxury not to do without, unless you can afford lithium.

Though they are the least expensive, standard or heavy-duty carbon-zinc batteries have about one-fourth the life of alkaline batteries.

In buying bulbs be aware that the smaller the number of the bulb, the more current it draws. For example, an alkaline D battery will last about 11.8 hours when used with a PR2 bulb. With a PR4 bulb it will last about 30.3 hours. As a general rule, the smallest bulb with sufficient light for general use around camp is the PR6.

Assembling the First-Aid Kit

A few often-forgotten items that should go into every outdoor first-aid kit: a couple of women's pads for either the unexpected or as an ideal pressure bandage; latex—never plastic—gloves for treating injuries involving blood; a first-aid pamphlet, this one from the Skagit Mountain Rescue Unit, Box 2, Mount Vernon, WA 98273; and a couple of glove warming packs, popular with skiers to help in cases of hypothermia.

There is a significant difference between first aid and treating a medical problem in the wilderness. First aid is temporary help you can give a sick or injured person until an ambulance or qualified medical personnel arrive. Wilderness medicine is what may touch on actual medical practice because help may be hours, or even days, away. Unless you have studied wilderness medicine, the least that is required of a trip leader is a course in first aid. These are widely available through every chapter of the American Red Cross.

In putting together a first-aid kit for a family or a group, start with a waterproof container, clearly labeled with red crosses painted with nail polish. The first item that goes into it: a first-aid guide. I recommend any of the following booklets: *Wilderness Medicine* by Dr. William Forgey, available from the American Canoe Association Bookservice, P.O. Box 1190, Newington, VA 22122-1190; *Mountaineering Medicine* by Dr. Fred Darvill, available from the Skagit Mountain Rescue Unit, Box 2, Mount Vernon, WA 98273; and *Emergency Survival Handbook* by the American Outdoor Safety League, available through the Appalachian Trail Conference, P.O. Box 807, Dept. SD, Harpers Ferry, WV 25425.

Second: a pair of latex gloves, worn when treating an injury where there is blood.

When considering what else goes into your kit, here are the items I carry on a major wilderness outing of a week or longer, whether I'm with our small family of 4, or a 10-person group:

Sharp, pointed small scissors.

Two rolls of adhesive tape, one broad, one narrow.

Band-Aids. Bring plenty. Kids enjoy wearing the colorful kind.

Adhesive butterfly dressings to hold together the edges of a wound that may have to be stitched by a surgeon.

Sterile 3-by-3 gauze pads.

A roll of 2-inch sterile gauze bandage.

A roll of 3-inch Ace bandage.

Heavy moleskin to cover foot sores and blisters.

Hypohyperthermia thermometer, which registers temperatures from the mid-70s to the 100s F. Especially important when checking the temperature of a person believed suffering from hypothermia.

A few single-edge razor blades.

Tweezers. Those with a built-in magnifying glass are helpful in pulling out almost invisible slivers.

A large sewing needle for digging out big slivers.

Over-the-counter cold medication.

A tube of sterile Vaseline.

Toothache medication.

Pain reliever, e.g., aspirin, ibuprofen, Aleve, Tylenol.

Sore-throat lozenges.

A few swab sticks.

Fingernail clippers.

Safety pins, large.

Several Kotex pads. These are excellent as pressure bandages as well as for feminine hygiene.

A small plastic bottle of rubbing alcohol (isopropyl) for cleansing instruments or wiping skin clean.

Over-the-counter drugs to control diarrhea and as a laxative, and Benadryl to reduce reaction to insect bites.

Several chemical packages of hand warmers used by skiers. These are instantly useful for treating hypothermia.

And finally, a small roll of unopened paper towels, any brand. The paper is as sterile as a sterile bandage before it is opened.

When we're not traveling, the first-aid box sits atop our refrigerator for the usual household emergencies.

WHICH PRESCRIPTION DRUGS SHOULD YOU INCLUDE?

In a wilderness situation, it is necessary to have on hand prescription medicine—*and a complete description by the physician who prescribed them on when and how they should be administered.* Among these are:

An antihistamine for violent reaction to poison plants, insects, or food.

A broad-range antibiotic for treating a major infection.

A prescription medication to induce sleep.

A medication to control hysteria.

An anti-exhaustion drug if it is critical to postpone rest because of an emergency.

A strong painkiller.

A medication for treating eye infections or to reduce eye pain as a result of lengthy exposure to brilliant sun.

Prescription drugs for treating major diarrhea or constipation.

It is especially important to talk to your pediatrician or family doctor before taking youngsters under the age of 12 on a wilderness outing. She may suggest medication specifically for your children.

As mentioned previously, adults should be able to administer artificial respiration and treat hypothermia if involved in canoeing or winter camping and cross-country skiing.

Foiling the Koosy-Oonek

We all know a trail companion who always has some totally unnecessary object in his pack. And when we spot it we ask ourselves: "Whyinthehell would he, or she (as the case may be), carry that?"

There is, by way of an absurd example, a close friend who adds to his gear an ancient Swiss Army knife with 38 attachments, which I have never seen him use. But his explanation for it: "One of the attachments may come in handy."

Horace Kephart, author of *The Book of Camping and Woodcraft,* published almost 100 years ago, also noted "that amusing foible, common to us all of lugging a useless object, from a broken mouth harp to a shaving mug."

He said, "If you have some such thing that you know you can't sleep well without, stow it religiously in your kit. It is your 'medicine,' your amulet against the spooks and bogies of the woods. It will dispel the Koosy-Oonek.

"If you don't know what that means, ask an Eskimo. He may tell you that it means sorcery, witchcraft—and so, no doubt, it does to the children of nature; but to us children of guile it is the spell of that imp who hides our pipes, steals our last match, and brings rain on the just when they want to go fishing."

Kephart said his amulet was "a porcelain teacup, minus the handle. . . . Many's the gibe I have suffered for its dear sake. But I do love it. Hot indeed must be the sun, tangled the trail, and weary the miles before I forsake thee, O my frail, cool-lipped, but ardent teacup!"

Aha. Now you have discovered the secret of how to foil that woodland ghoul who drags your shoes outside the tent the night it rains, turns on your flashlight after you put it in your pack, and tips the soup over when you add a couple of pieces of wood to the fire. My amulet is a small, scratched shaving mirror that still has printed on the back an ancient advertisement: "Venable Lumber Co., Phone SKyline 3-3411."

No matter what your talisman is, pack it along with you.

The Koosy-Oonek will never disturb your camping adventures again.

Packing Tips

- Toss a bottle of red nail polish into your pack. Use it to paint initials on cups and bowls; to make Xs on a medical kit. You'll find many uses for identification purposes.
- Sometime in the 1930s The Mountaineers, an outdoor and conservation organization founded in 1906 in Seattle, published this list of "The Ten Essentials for Backpackers": appropriate trail map, compass, extra clothing including rain gear, fire starter, matches, sunglasses and sunscreen, extra food, knife, first-aid kit, and flashlight. The list is still valid.

- Pack four essentials if stopping at a motel en route to your wilderness destination: a self-stick hook to attach to the inside of the bathroom door so you can hang something up, two large safety pins for holding the window drapes together, and a 100-watt bulb to replace the chintzy ones in the room.
- An angler's filleting knife with a built-in sharpener in the scabbard always means a sharp knife in your camp kitchen.
- It's as important to have critical first-aid materials with you if you travel alone as it is to have a complete first-aid kit when traveling with a group.
- Print your name, address, and telephone number on iron-on tags for your backpack, sleeping bag, tent, airline bag, camera bag, and, if you still carry them, suitcases.
- When repacking foods to get rid of the boxes, use Ziploc plastic bags. They are waterproof, lightweight, and reusable.
- A shaving brush is the best friend the well-shaven outdoorsman can carry. Even a tiny cake of soap taken from the motel you stopped at on your way to the trailhead will stir up a fine froth of foam to ease shaving when applied with a brush. Remember, aftershave lotion odors are a clarion call of assembly for mosquitoes.
- When backpacking, leave the valuables at home.
- In the vastness of the wilderness there is ample space for all the sounds and sights of nature, but not a spare inch for a boombox or portable TV.

5

Setting Out on the Trail

Happily may I walk,
May it be beautiful before me.
May it be beautiful behind me.
May it be beautiful below me.
May it be beautiful above me.
May it be beautiful all around me.
In beauty it is finished.
    —*Navajo*

The Verbal Outing (Or How to Speak "Wildernese")

Among the subtle joys of heading into the wilds is the opportunity to talk to your companions about the pleasures of exchanging crowded cities and tense work, hostile drivers and overextended credit cards, for the solitude of river and mountain, of too much weight stuffed into your sturdy backpack, and the excitement of spotting a sloth of bears on the far side of the canyon.

A sloth of bears?

Of course. Would you call a group of bears a cluster? A litter? A herd? Maybe a swarm?

Indeed not.

But unless you are familiar with the poetry of traditional group names for birds, beasts, fish, and even people, you may not be aware that two of the first books printed in English were *The Egerton Manuscript*, in 1450, followed in 1486 by *The Book of St. Albans*. Both were basically

From St. Alban's Lists

A host of sparrows.

A tiding of magpies.

A parliament of owls.

A drift of fishermen.

A covey of partridges.

A watch of nightingales.

A flight of swallows.

A route of wolves.

A dray of squirrels.

A nest of rabbits.

A clowder of cats.

A clutch of eggs.

A siege of herons.

A bouquet of pheasants.

A spring of teal.

A cast of hawks.

An army of caterpillars.

A fall of woodcocks.

A skulk of foxes.

A stalk of foresters.

A knot of toads.

A mustering of storks.

codified lists of group names that the well educated were expected to know.

Many are still in use. All are yours to add to your lexicon of the wilds. Both for your own pleasure and to amuse and amaze your friends. By way of example: A cluster of fish is a school of fish. Naturally, you knew that. What if they are all trout? Call them a "hover of trout." Or all bass? A "shoal of bass." A mob of people at an adjacent campsite? A "congregation of people."

If they are on the water, it's a "gaggle of geese," or a "paddling of ducks." In flight, both are referred to as a "skein" of geese or of ducks.

In one way or another, all those bright Middle English terms began with some reference to characteristics or life patterns, such as:

A colony of ants.

A swarm of bees.

A plague of locusts.

A murder of crows.

A murmuration of starlings.

An unkindness of ravens.

A rafter of turkeys.

And a group of various birds? A dissimulation.

Al were at one time in general use. All are equally delightful and valid today. And quite appropriate for such use as would add a melody to your words. Enjoy each encounter.

Courtesy on the Trail

Each of us has a personal responsibility when traveling in the wilderness, whether by foot, four-wheeler, bike, or pack train, to exercise good trail behavior.

This includes such things as staying on the trail. If it's a switchback, the sensitive traveler will not tear up terrain by cutting across from loop to loop and ripping open new segments of trail, which can suffer from erosion.

While meeting horses on the trail is a rarity today, if you do encounter them step several feet to one side and wait quietly until they pass.

A typical Adirondack shelter, three sides, sloping roof, open front, with stone fireplace. In heavily used areas, the shelter will include a sturdy wood table and benches. It is a common courtesy for early arrivals to share the quarters with latecomers—when there is room.

A descent of woodpeckers.
A string of ponies.
A gang of elk.
A bale of turtles.
A labor of moles.
A singular of boars.
A charm of finches.
A blast of hunters.
An incredulity of cuckolds.
A drift of hogs.
A cete of badgers.
A congregation of plovers.
A walk of snipe.
A richness of martens.
A cowardice of curs.
A trip of goats.
A sounder of swine.
A harras of horses.
A cluster of knots.
A rag of colts.
A deceit of lapwings.
An ostentation of peacocks.
An exaltation of larks.

How to Estimate Back-packing Travel Time

Unless you actually know the trail, or have read detailed accounts of your planned trip in the rich variety of books and pamphlets that cover almost every trail in every section of the United States, and an amazing number in countries throughout the world, here are three things to consider in figuring backpacking time.

Item 1: The terrain.

Item 2: The actual distance planned as measured on a topographic map, not "as the bird flies" distance from point A to point B.

Item 3: The hiking ability of those in your party.

With these three items calculated (depending, naturally, upon what a howling mountain storm can do to your travel plans), you should be able to gauge with remarkable accuracy how far your group will travel per day or per week.

Let's look at Item 1. Know the terrain! Is it rocky, covered with scree, or swampy? What will this do to travel plans? If at high altitudes, say above 7,000 feet, do you anticipate going slower than normal while everyone adjusts to the elevation? Is it reasonably flat or mountainous?

Now, Item 2. First, measure the actual mileage planned on your topographic map. In addition to estimating time to cover the miles on a flat course, add one additional hour for each 1,000-foot change in elevation. Thus, if on one day you will be climbing and descending a 500-foot ridge, and then a 1,000-foot peak because the view from the summit is spectacular, add three hours to estimated hiking time for distance.

Item 3. On level ground, without carrying a loaded pack, the average person walking at a steady, reasonably brisk pace will cover about 3 miles an hour. Add a loaded backpack, turn the sidewalk into a rocky mountain trail that goes up and down hills, and the rate of travel is far more apt to be 1 or 2 miles an hour than 3.

So in a nonstop sidewalk trek of five hours, without pack or slowing down, the distance covered is 15 miles. Now make that five hours of backpacking in the mountains, with time out to rest on steep pitches and for lunch, and how far will you travel? Six, 7 miles?

It is important to understand how many miles you and your companions probably will cover when planning an enjoyable journey—loaded with tents, extra clothes, food, and only those additional items that are actually essential in the wilderness. Of course, there are groups in the wilderness that have no hesitation letting the stronger and faster hike on ahead, and the slower and weaker straggle behind. This can lead to disaster, especially with the stragglers. Something goes awry. They take the wrong fork in the trail and get lost when night blankets the valley. A fall. A broken leg. Whatever it is, help is needed.

I follow an absolute policy on all my wilderness trips, whether by canoe or afoot. We travel no faster than the slowest, weakest members of the party. We have a "lead" hiker or canoe, and a strong "sweep" hiker or canoe. No one passes lead. No one drops in back of sweep. If one stops, we all stop.

Plan each trail trek based upon the slowest in your group, whether friends or family.

How (and Why) to Pace Yourself

Rhythm.

Whether dancing or backpacking, rhythm is a significant factor to put into the way you go from step to step to step. My own awareness of "backpacking" pacing began in the army. It was then I realized that a steady pace that could be maintained from morning until the end of the day was the way the army traveled.

Not so Boy Scout Troop 402, a newly organized group of eager young Scouts who leaped into action at the outset of our first weekend backpacking trip.

Quick. Let's go, guys. Come on.

But, this Scoutmaster observed, the ardent enthusiasm soon faded. After a couple of hours, the outburst of speed had slowed remarkably. By the end of the day, butts were dragging.

This is equally true of inexperienced adults who take to the trails. Novices are anxious to start off quickly, then slow, then drag, then collapse. Veterans have learned that a casual pace is the way to hike hour after hour. No outburst of speed. When traveling with a group, begin at a trail gait that is comfortable for the slowest. Let your walking become automatically casual. Don't let it even enter your consciousness that you and your trail friends are hiking too fast, or too slow. Of course, a sudden change in the weather could change all that.

The rhythm of trail hiking slows at high altitudes. When backpacking above 7,000 feet, it is wisdom, indeed, to set an even slower pace than at lower elevations—one you can maintain through the day. No rush. Let the body adjust to the higher altitude. If it takes two or three days, so be it. Take elevation into account when planning how far you will carry the weight of that backpack before you start.

Women's Room, Men's Room

The experienced have an infallible system for who goes where when the group makes a pit stop. The women hike up the trail, the men walk back down when searching for a hidden cat hole. You'll never forget this system: Women go up because they pull their dresses up; men go back down because they pull their pants down.

At the same time, be army. Hike for a reasonable time, then take a break. The army rests 10 minutes out of every hour. The regularly scheduled breaks ease the hiking pressure. It is equally true on your backpacking journeys.

So do!

Straighten Your Footstep

The average step is made with our feet angled slightly outward. If your foot is straight forward on each step, then each step will be a fraction of an inch longer. Not much difference in an hour, but fractions mount after thousands of steps. Keep your feet parallel.

Resupply on the Trail

Experienced backpackers are fully aware that the weight of the pack grinding into their backs the day they start putting one boot in front of the other isn't going to drop by a single ounce on the trail except for one item—food.

Even by basing meals on dry cereals, freeze-dried and dehydrated foods, the weight of all the calories they carry will be around 2 pounds per day. One week: 15 pounds. Two weeks: 30 pounds. How many weeks of hiking through swamps and up hills can your back tote to start?

When a trail passes near or goes through towns, stop off and do some grocery shopping. Meals of store-bought groceries are likely to average out to about 3 pounds a day. However, light foods planned in advance can be mailed to a post office near the trail, along with those fresh hiking socks and other small essentials. Joe Gohikem mails his to: Joe Gohikem, c/o General Delivery, local post office. Mark it: "Please hold for addressee arriving about [date]."

Another technique to reequip or resupply the hiker depends on a friend who will drive to a prearranged site to meet Joe and bring the chosen delectables. Joe also can take several packs of food and drive to areas along the trail where they can be hidden until he comes hiking through.

Backpacking with Kids

Backpacking with the children is a family adventure. But it also can be an adventure with whining and tears for the unprepared. The solution: Anticipate, and go prepared.

The first step: Make certain they have appropriate clothes to walk in, comfortable shoes, and their own pack in which they can stuff a few camp as well as favorite personal items to carry on the trail. Just like their parents do.

WHINE BUSTERS FOR THE YOUNG (AND YOUNG AT HEART)

Kids, especially, the youngest, have short interest spans. So add lively moments when hiking along.

Hear a bird? Stop. Point. "Where is it? If we see it maybe we can identify it. Let's try and find it in our bird book." Which of course you can do if you actually carry a small book with color pictures of birds common to the area you are in.

Take frequent breaks so youngsters are not pushed to exhaustion. Use these to search for something special: A mushroom. A prize to the first one who sees a butterfly. Or a caterpillar. Take off their shoes, check the feet for blisters, then let them splash in the stream.

Bring along a point-and-shoot camera. Help those who need a helping hand to take their own choice of pictures.

On little-traveled sections, encourage kids to do what they excel at: make noise, sing, shout, bang cups together. Explain they are doing this to alert animals and frighten away those that might be dangerous.

Naturally everyone, including the kids, will enjoy some healthy goodies tucked in their pack, which they have the freedom to reach in and gobble, whether walking or resting, whenever they want. A great snack is GORP: Good Old Raisins and Peanuts. Mix your own combination of nuts, raisins, chopped dried fruits, and such candy bits as M&Ms.

Search for edible berries. What a pleasure to stop and pick and eat. Spot a cave. Let them explore it.

Above all, make backpacking a fun experience for everyone, even for the child who ends up in your arms because she's just too tired to walk any farther.

ACTIVITIES FOR TEENS

Campers needn't worry about older kids who will become restless hanging around with "nothin' to do" unless you drag along a portable television set, a boombox, or something from cyberspace to destroy the challenge, the quiet, the power of simply understanding the nature of nature. Here are a few teen-friendly suggestions to enrich their wilderness adventure.

The Map Challenge: For older novices, bring along a large-scale contour map and a compass. Let them see for themselves how the drawings on the map precisely picture the land they are walking on. And how to use a compass to orient the map.

Before challenging that towering wilderness cliff, test your nerve, fingers, and toes on an indoor climbing wall.

Make a friendly game out of map reading. For those who have learned well, encourage them to take the lead. Stop from time to time and ask them to put their finger on the exact spot where you are all standing.

Rock Climbing: Unless you are an experienced climber, you'll want to arm yourself with carabiners, proper rope, a few climbing gadgets, and the fundamental knowledge found in *Basic Mountaineering*, published by the Sierra Club. It would be even more helpful if you and all potential climbers first practice an ascent on one or more of the widely available indoor climbing walls.

Panning for Gold: Traveling alongside a stream? Send your teens out to pan for gold. Who knows, they may dredge up enough flecks to pay for your vacation, or for their college education.

If you forgot to buy a commercially available gold pan, an old frying pan—from 10 to 12 inches in diameter, with sides from 2 to 2½ inches deep—will do quite well for imitating what the early gold miners did.

The old prospectors would fill their pan with black sand, then slowly submerge it in 6 to 12 inches of quiet water. Then the muck in the pan was carefully kneaded until all the lumps were broken. The pan was held flat underwater and shaken until the mud was washed off. Next came the critical step: The pan was tilted and raised quickly, still underwater, in a circular motion to swish away the light material on the surface. This dip, tilt, swish-and-raise-swiftly was repeated until nothing was left on the bottom but heavy minerals and, aha, *flecks of gold.*

If the prospecting family comes home with a poke, warning: Shut up—until you know the laws.

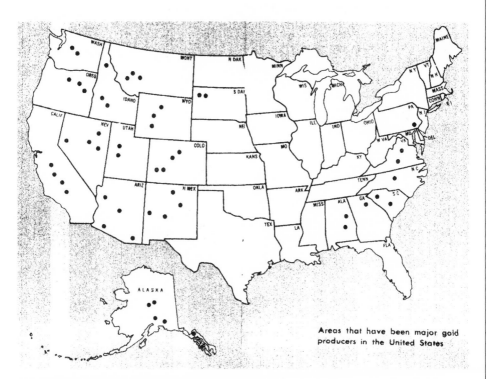

Areas that have been major gold producers in the United States

A Geological Survey map shows principal gold-producing areas in the United States.

Both federal and state laws are quite rigid and complex about finding and selling gold. Yes, prospecting is legal, and you can sell those gold smidgens if you follow the juridical convolutions involved.

For comprehensive information read the Bureau of Mines Information Circular 8517: *How to Mine and Prospect for Placer Gold.* It is available through the Superintendent of Documents, U.S. Government Printing Office, Washington, DC 20402.

You'll have the greatest luck panning for gold in any area where gold has been found or gold mines still exist. Hunt along creeks and rivers where the shore sand is black. Dig deep. Fill your pan. If you don't hit it big—try a lottery ticket.

Whistle Insurance

If there is a single item every child (and every parent) should carry, it is a whistle. If lost, children should blow on it. Someone hunting for them may hear it. If they hear a whistle, they should wipe the tears from their eyes and blow on their own whistle. Help will be at their side quickly.

"WHAT IF I GET LOST?"

One of the strongest fears a child may have is: "What happens if I get lost?"

Always explain to younger children that because they could get lost in the woods, they are not to leave camp at any time. For the older ones, it is mandatory that they do not leave camp without telling you where they are going and when they will be back.

What happens if they do get lost? Well, as a friend once said, his advice to the young ones was simple: "Listen, if you get lost in the woods come straight back to camp."

Explain to the children that if they do get lost, they are not to run around looking for camp. Stay where they are. Find someplace to sleep if they are not found before dark.

Play "I'm lost" games when hiking. Tell them they are lost right where you now stand. Emphasize that when they do not return to camp, someone will be looking for them. If they have to spend the night in the woods, what can they find for protection? Is there a cave nearby? Can they crawl into a depression and cover themselves with bundles of leaves until morning? Teach them survival before they have forgotten where the camp is.

Backpacking with the Family Dog

A dog can be your closest friend on a backpacking trip. But if he's like all city folk, he'll be a better friend if he's conditioned to scramble along mountain trails before he ever sets his paws on one.

So let him join in your own preconditioning. Let him walk on sidewalks and rough park paths on your daily stint. Only when he, and his feet, are in as good a physical shape as you are is he ready for that outing expedition.

PET-FRIENDLY TRAVEL TIPS

Be sure to take care of little details in advance. Will your Fido be permitted in the campgrounds? Most camp areas permit dogs if they are kept on a leash. Some require proof of inoculation against rabies. Lacking such proof, are you aware that if she takes a nip out of some unsuspecting leg and there is suspicion of rabies she could have her head summarily removed and sent to a laboratory for examination?

When making hotel or motel reservations, ask if they accept pets. The AAA has information on establishments that do.

Make certain he wears a metal identification tag. Even a normally placid gentleman can become excited and jump out of a car, or get lost chasing an imaginary rabbit in the woods.

If possible, the food should be the same your dog is accustomed to at home. On the trail, she can carry it in a dog pannier. A sturdy dog can carry up to 25 percent of her body weight, according to Mark Yerkees, director of Urban Programs and Outdoor Leadership with the Appalachian Mountain Club.

City dogs need conditioning, especially a toughening of their feet, before joining their masters in wilderness travel. In canoes, dogs need the protection of canine life vests. An easy weekend trip with Mr. Mutt will give both of you an idea of what's in store when he shares tent, trail, and canoe.

QUILLS, SPILLS, AND OTHER DOGGIE DILEMMAS

A pannier stuffed with Ping Pong balls is a fine lifesaver should your dog spill overboard while canoeing. However, the greatest danger a canoeist faces with a dog is that about the time the nose of the canoe edges into the bank, the dog leaps into the water, then welcomes his master ashore with muddy feet.

For campers who fear their dog may get giardiasis lapping up stream water or puddles, this is no cause for concern. Dr. Chuck Hibler of CH Diagnostics in Fort Collins, Colorado, says the organism is present in almost every dog he's ever examined, and the dog suffers no ill effects.

Out of simple curiosity, a city dog may tangle once with a skunk and once with a porcupine. Quills in the nose or cheeks of a howling dog usually can be pulled out by hand or pushed through the skin into the mouth. Do not let the barbs work their way into the dog's body.

As for a dog sprayed by the delicate odor of skunk, there really is no truly effective way to rid her of it. Some recommend washing with vinegar, tomato juice, or a dishwashing liquid without bleach. Or tie her downwind until the odor dwindles to a memory.

When in camp, examine your dog nightly for ticks. Pull them out. Dot the spot with antibiotic. Matted hairs from burrs in the ears or on the feet are painful and should be cut off with scissors. Doggie booties are great protection against sore, torn, or bleeding pads.

First aid for the camper scamper usually consists of treating a wound from a confrontation with another dog or animal. Wash the wound with Epsom salts. Serious injuries require veterinarian care.

Backpacking Tips

- Keep a diary and take pictures on every wilderness outing. Write names and dates on the back of all photographs.
- Friends on the trail come in every color, race, religion, nationality, political faith, sexual persuasion, and age.
- Falling in love is more exciting on a camping trip than in a bar.
- Feet aching from blisters when trail hiking? Army medical researchers say that antiperspirants applied to feet will help prevent them. They found that the rubbing of a shoe against dry skin produced less friction than rubbing against moist skin.

6

Setting Out on the Water

O Shenandoah, I long to hear you,
Way-hay, you rolling river!
O Shenandoah, I long to hear you,
Way-hay, we're bound away,
Cross the wide Missouri!
   —Anonymous

The Contemporary Canoe

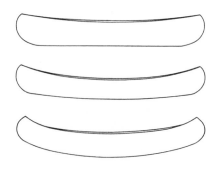

There are three fundamental hull shapes: The flat is popular for cruising; the moderate rocker for combination cruising and maneuvering; and the extreme rocker for heavy white-water paddling.

A magnificent example of a hand-built wooden canoe.

Those beautiful hand-made wooden canoes that generations ago replaced birch-bark canoes themselves were replaced after World War II by canoes made of aluminum, followed by today's engineer-designed models made of such modern products as fiberglass, ABS (acrylonitrile-butadiene-styrene), polyethylene (a plastic resin), and Kevlar 49, (ounce for ounce five times stronger than steel).

The average widely available 16-foot canoes made of fiberglass, ABS, or polyethylene will bow your shoulders with a weight of approximately 75 pounds when totting one across a portage. The Kevlar 49 will weigh in at around 45 to 50 pounds. Ah, science.

Choosing the Right-Sized Paddle

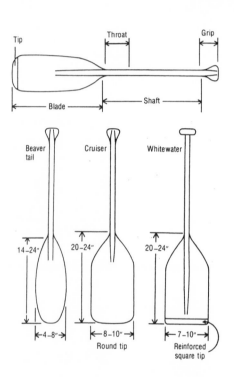

The parts of the paddle, and three basic shapes. A fourth shape found today is bent at an angle where the blade attaches to the shaft. It is highly effective in flat water, but not for maneuvering rapids. In the past, New Englanders favored ash paddles, once carved from a single piece of wood. Echoes of an earlier era can be heard today when a Maine canoeist yells to his partner: "Lay 'er to the ash!" Meaning, paddle harder.

Livery canoes come equipped with paddles of two sizes: too long and too short. A rough guide to length is to look for a paddle that comes somewhere between your chin and forehead when held vertically, with the blade on the ground. When in doubt, use a slightly shorter paddle in the bow, a slightly longer one in the stern.

The two items that avid beginning paddlers first buy are their own paddle and a PFD.

Before buying a paddle, accurately measure your preferred paddle length. Sit in a canoe in the water. Grasp a paddle handle with one hand and hold it level with your shoulder. Place your bottom hand on the shaft, held vertically, at the water level. This is the point where the blade actually begins. Now add to the distance between your two hands the length of your choice of blade. Ergo: This paddle length is an all-around fit for you. The popular tulip-shaped blade is 8 to 10 inches wide and 20 to 24 inches long.

Obviously, experienced canoeists, as with tennis players and anglers, never settle for the one and only. There will be two or three or four hanging in a cool, dark place, slightly different in length and blade, each impatiently waiting for the next trip.

Always slip an extra paddle into your canoe. Paddles do get broken or lost in an upset.

How to Locate Liveries and Outfitters

Two outstanding sources for locating canoe, kayak, and sea kayak liveries, as well as wilderness outfitters throughout the 50 United States are:

Paddle America, by Nick and David Shears, a guide to more than 870 canoe, kayak, and sea kayak liveries in all 50 states, published by Starfish Press, P.O. Box 42467, Washington, DC; tel: 202-244-7827. It provides an excellent description of the waters served by each livery.

Protecting the Six-Pack (A Gentle Gibe)

Why suffer wearing a personal flotation device, otherwise known as a PFD, or a life jacket, on a muggy summer day when you can cool off while using yours to protect a six-pack towed in the cool water behind the canoe.?If the canoe flips, at least the pack will be rescued.

Question: How can you differentiate between veteran and novice paddlers at the livery put in-where the water is alive with canoeists starting down the river.
Answer: Obviously the novices know something the veterans don't. They sit on their PFDs. The veterans wear theirs.

The North American Paddlesports Association, Jim Thaxton, executive director. For a list of the several hundred livery members, which are subject to inspections to assure that they maintain the high safety and service standards of the NAPA, contact the NAPA at RR2, Box 248, Butler, KY 41006; tel: 606-472-2205.

P.S. Paddle America contributes 10 percent of its net profits from sale of the book to American Rivers, the nation's leading river conservation organization.

A word of caution: When dealing with an unknown livery, always check in advance as to its rain check policy in the event of a storm, or exceptionally high and dangerous or unusually low water.

Pointers for Renting Canoes

Since few wilderness paddlers actually own their own canoes, they usually rent from a canoe livery or wilderness outfitter. Make certain you know in advance what kind of canoes they rent you.

Examine a rental canoe carefully, especially an older one. Put it in the water at the livery site and paddle around for 10 or 15 minutes. Don't accept it if you have any doubts. On one trip in the wilds of northwestern Quebec, one rental canoe in our party began developing leaks the first day where the livery operate had poorly patched a leaking seam with duct tape. We resealed it daily for the next 10 days.

Here are some other points to consider in renting: Does the canoe rental fee include an extra paddle and life jackets for each paddler, or are these supplied only for an additional fee? Do you get a rain check if foul weather cancels your trip? Does the livery accept credit cards? Which ones? If you are in a foreign country and expect to pay in dollars, what is the livery's rate of exchange?

Paddling Colleges

Other sports besides football, baseball, and basketball are winning advocates in today's colleges and universities, such as both competition in canoe and kayak races, and taking these sports up through school programs for the joy and sweet excitement of simply paddling. Here are some of the nation's outstanding paddling colleges as rated by *Paddler* magazine: Idaho State University, Pocatello; University of Montana, Missoula; University of Washington, Seattle; University of Minnesota, Duluth; Dartmouth College, Hanover, New Hampshire; Georgia State University, Atlanta; Paul Smith College, Paul Smith, New York; and University of Tennessee, Knoxville.

Estimating Canoe Travel Time

In planning a wilderness canoe trip it is common sense to know the skill and ability of every member of your group. With that knowledge you can plan a great experience that everyone will enjoy.

This chart may help you; in it, you'll find typical distances with two adults paddling tandem about five hours daily. It is only a guide and can be affected by weather, water levels, and whether you will be paddling with or against prevailing winds. The assumption is that you will be paddling waters at

Lake	River 1–3 mph	River-lake	River 3–5 mph
No portages, current	No portages	Mild currents, 1-mile portage	1–2 short portages daily
Novices & low intermediates			
8–12 miles	12–18 miles	10–15 miles	10+ miles
Strong intermediates			
12–18 miles	18–20 miles	15+ miles	20+ miles
Experts			
15–20+ miles	20+ miles	20+ miles	20+ miles

medium, or M, level, and portage distances over relatively easy terrain of no more than ¼ mile each.

Since few recreational canoeists have developed the specific muscles needed for paddling, plan shorter distances the first few days. The paddlers who have trouble with a minimum distance the first couple of days will be charging across the water like veterans at the end of a two-week wilderness junket.

In estimating total trip time, plan on one full-day layover each week, usually somewhere around the third to fifth day after put-in. These should be days with a minimum of formal plans except for setting out a lazy food menu that requires the least amount of preparation, especially for breakfast and lunch, washing socks, airing sleeping pads, or doing what comes naturally.

Courtesy on the Water

Even paddlers must exercise courtesy on the water. It simply is not polite to paddle a canoe under a fisherman's pole, or to bump into him, even if accidentally, while trying to steer past. When canoeing rocky or rough water, the paddler ahead of you has priority both for courtesy and safety. Do not crowd him if he slows down while maneuvering through swift current. Be polite. Bumping into him could knock his canoe off course, or cause your canoe to flip.

Professional versus Amateur Rafting

Rafting comes in two sizes: professional and amateur. The wild, electrifying scenes on TV of rafts bouncing through massive sets of rapids with six or eight people aboard, clinging for life to the raft, is a sport operated by skilled professionals. What you won't see on the sports newscasts are small rafts with four or six people aboard, from kiddies tucked into life jackets to cheerful grandparents, paddling down far tamer rivers alongside open canoes. This is rafting operated by the amateurs sitting in the raft.

Professional rafting is an expensive, thrilling way of challenging rivers with great sets of rapids. Depending on the river, of course, rafting trips may run from one day to a couple of weeks. On trips of more than a day, outfitters generally provide everything, from meals and tents to wet suits in chill weather.

Amateur rafters rent their craft from liveries, which are found along rivers throughout the nation. In addition to rafts, liveries provide life jackets, paddles, and some suggestions on how to free a raft stuck on rocks. Those aboard bring whatever else they want. About the only danger these rafters face is figuring out what to do when it rains and their takeout livery is still an hour away.

Easy river rafting is a tremendously popular weekend sport. On the nationally designated 75-mile scenic section of the Delaware River, an estimated 7,000 weekend adventurers go rafting on a pleasant weekend day. This is probably as many as the total number being shepherded down wild rapids by professional guides throughout the entire United States at the same time.

Rating Rivers, Paddlers, and Water Levels

Rapids on rivers vary in their intensity. Take note of the common sense of experienced paddlers: None ever plan a river trip without being aware of the wildness of the rapids and whether or not they have the skill to paddle them, or without knowing the length of portages around rapids they cannot handle.

TO RUN, OR NOT TO RUN?

The International Rating System classifies rapids as follows:

Class A: Lake water. No perceptible movement.

Class I: Easy, smooth river water; light riffles; clear passages, occasional sandbars, and gentle curves.

Class II: Moderate. Medium-quick water; rapids with regular waves; clear and open passages between rocks and ledges. Maneuvering and "reading" water required. Best handled by intermediate paddlers.

Class III: Difficult. Numerous high and irregular waves; rocks and eddies with passages clear but narrow. For expert paddlers. Visual inspection required if rapids are unknown. Canoes without flotation bags may have problems.

Class IV: Very difficult. Long and powerful rapids and standing waves, souse holes and boiling eddies. Precise maneuvering required. Visual inspection mandatory. For kayaks, rafts, or white-water canoes with flotation bags. Advance preparation for possible rescue important. Cannot be run by open canoes.

Class V: Extremely difficult. Long and violent rapids that follow each other without interruption. Big drops and violent currents. For rafts and top experts in kayaks or white-water canoes with flotation bags only. Advance preparation for possible rescue important.

Class VI: Violent and turbulent water, steep drops. Navigable only when water levels and conditions favorable. Only for paddlers in kayaks and white-water canoes with flotation bags; constant threat of death. For rafts controlled by experts. For paddlers of Olympic ability only.

A River Folk Song

(To the tune of "The Wreck of the Old '97")

Oh they gave him his orders at old Narrowsburg saying: "Steve, you're way behind time.

"This ain't an ABS. It's a beat-up old Gruman. Just get her into Jervis on time."

So he turned and he said to his golden-haired partner: "Baby make those muscles roll.

"And when we hit those Barryville rapids you will see this Gruman really stroll."

They were going through the rapids making 90 miles an hour when his partner broke into a scream.

They were found in the wreck of that beat-up old Gruman a-drownded to death by the stream.

Oh gather around, all you fair ladies, from this time on and learn:

Never make out with your partner in the Barryville rapids—you may flip and never return.

DON'T GET IN OVER YOUR HEAD

The characteristics of rapids can change remarkably as the waters of a river rise or fall. A set of Class II rapids can turn into Class IV in a heavy spring runoff, or a shallow pussycat in late summer.

An International Rating System describes the change in water levels and rate of flow, which also affects the rating of rapids. Here is how the IRS describes rivers:

L, or Low. Below normal for the river. Usually indicates problems for paddlers because shallows turn into sandbars.

M, or Medium. Normal river flow. Medium usually means good canoeing water for rivers.

H, or High. Water above normal stage. Paddlers may refer to H water as "heavy." Small debris may come floating by. The river could be dangerous and is best left to rafts, kayaks, and white-water canoes.

HH, or High-High. Very heavy water. Hydraulics are complex. Slight gradients become treacherous. Debris frequent. Only for experts.

F, or Flood. Abnormally high water overflowing the banks. Low-lying areas underwater. Trees and shreds of buildings come floating by. TV crews shoot tape for the evening news from helicopters. Only for boaters with appropriate equipment on dangerous rescue missions.

CAN U CANOE?

Obviously, it is not enough to rate the rapids and water levels without rating the skill levels of paddlers as well. Here is how the Appalachian Mountain Club rates canoeists and kayakers:

Class I: Beginner. Is familiar with basic strokes and can handle a tandem canoe competently from the bow or stern in Class I water; solo canoeist is familiar with basic strokes.

Class II: Novice. Can handle more advanced whitewater strokes solo or in either bow or stern of a tandem canoe. Knows how to read water; can negotiate easy and regular rapids with assurance.

Class III: Intermediate. Can negotiate rapids requiring linked sequence of maneuvers; understands and can use eddy turns and basic bow-upstream techniques; is skilled in either bow or stern of a tandem canoe; can paddle Class II rapids in a solo canoe or kayak.

Class IV: Expert. Has established ability to run difficult Class III and Class IV rapids in bow or stern of a tandem craft with appropriate flotation bags; can paddle solo in a properly equipped canoe or kayak; understands and can maneuver in H (High) water.

Class V: Leader. Is an expert canoeist; possesses the experience, judgment, and training to lead a group of any degree of skill on navigable waterways and in the wilderness.

Converting Canoes into Catamarans

Canoeists can take a well-deserved rest from paddling by erecting a sail—easily done in a tandem canoe. The bow paddler turns into a sail by standing up and holding a poncho between her outstretched hands. This leaves the stern paddler with nothing more strenuous to do than steer. Two canoes can convert their craft into a sailing catamaran by lashing them side by side with two poles or spare paddles, one fore, the other aft. The bows should have about 1 to 2 feet between them. The sterns should be at least 3 to 4 feet apart. This will keep water from piling up between the craft. Then, quite simply, the two bow paddlers stand up, stretching out ponchos as twin sails.

Finding and Selecting Portages

As every wilderness paddler knows, the steeper and more difficult the portage is, the harder it is raining when you take out.

Portages come in a weird variety of shapes and lengths. If you have done your homework, you have read, or talked to someone who knows, about the characteristics of all the portages on your proposed junket. And marked the exact location of each one on your topo map.

Once on the river you know, after checking your map, that the portage begins sort of over there. On seldom-paddled rivers, look for a small break in the vegetation growing along the shore, with obvious evidence of a trail beginning at the water's edge.

In keeping with a tradition as ancient as people carrying loads, that little break will probably be much closer to the water pounding through a major set of Class V rapids than you think reasonable. However, since Native Americans first carried that portage—running with their birch-bark canoes held aloft—they took the shortest distance between getting out of the water and back in. You don't have to run with your canoe.

On very short portages, perhaps 100 yards or less, a group carry is likely. Each canoe, without being unloaded, is carried across by four or six paddlers.

The quickest way to portage a loaded canoe through a short stretch of wilderness is the "all-hands" technique. However, if the stretch is much more than 100 yards, it's back to "each canoe for itself." Study large-scale maps of the trip you will paddle next summer. You should promptly get a bird's-eye view of the portages you may cross because of water too difficult to paddle, or the need to haul canoes, personal gear, community gear, and food a casual mile or two between bodies of water. Do you really need three pairs of socks in your pack?

Paddling on Open Water

On open water, paddlers must be wary of even a moderate breeze—which, in a surprisingly short time, can stir up running waves. The National Weather Service issues small-craft advisories when winds start frolicking at about 20 miles an hour, strong enough to sway small trees. When the waves develop whitecaps, keep an eye on the nearest shore. Or the lee side of an island. Unless you actually are skilled in paddling rough water, prepare to head for safety the moment the wind blows up a problem.

Better to light a candle in your tent ashore than to curse the darkness while bailing a canoe buffeted by winds.

How to Determine Wind Speeds

How strong the breeze? A scale, from 0 to 12, was devised by Admiral Sir Francis Beaufort of the British Navy about 1800 to judge wind velocity. It is the system the U.S. National Weather Service uses today. You can use it, too.

Hypothermia

In rainy or chilly weather, or after a fall into cold water, hypothermia may strike. Watch for telltale signs: excessive shivering, followed by an inability to paddle or walk, and finally unconsciousness. If possible, get the victim into dry clothes and under warm blankets. Immediately start warming the torso—not the arms and legs. Cover the head and apply warmth to the back, armpits, and stomach. Hospitalization is necessary to fully stabilize the victim.

Beaufort #

Speed of wind in mph

Beaufort #	Speed	Description	Specifications
0	less than 1	calm	smoke rises vertically
1	1–3	light air	wind direction shown by drift of smoke
2	4–7	slight breeze	wind felt on face, leaves rustle
3	8–12	gentle breeze	leaves, twigs in steady motion; wind extends light flags
4	13–18	moderate breeze	dust, loose paper, and small branches moved

5	19–24	fresh breeze	small, leafy trees begin to sway
6	25–31	strong breeze	large branches in motion; wires whistle
7	32–38	moderate gale	whole trees in motion
8	39–46	fresh gale	twigs beak off trees, walking is impeded
9	47–54	strong gale	light damage to houses, pots blown over
10	55–63	whole gale	trees uprooted, considerable damage to houses
11	64–75	storm	widespread damage
12	above 75	hurricane	extensive, major damage

Arriving Safe and Sound (Or Eventually Found)

Always make appropriate plans for what happens if you do not reach your takeout on the designated day. On the Sierra Club wilderness trips that I lead, I arrange for an outfitter to meet us. He is asked to notify the appropriate authorities to launch an aerial search if we do not arrive within 24 hours of the return date. Of course, he has a copy of our route on the topo maps we left with him.

Paddling Tips

- Prior to starting paddling down the river, biking a woodland trail, or trekking up a steep mountain, fill your water bottle and empty your bladder.
- For those who leave camp to paddle by themselves, start into the wind. Getting back will be a lot easier.

7

finding Your Way in the Wilderness

Afoot and light-hearted, I take to the open road,
Healthy, free, the world before me,
The long brown path before me leading wherever
I choose.
   —*Walt Whitman*
      1819–1892

Using the Global Positioning System

When you need to locate yourself, don't sweat it. GPS is a quick, efficient, reliable cyberspace method for determining where you are, whether backpacking a remote trail across the Tetons from Wyoming into Idaho, or trying to figure out how far it is at two o'clock on a stormy night driving to L. L. Bean in Freeport, Maine. For those who may need a bit of help in understanding GPS, the initials stand for Global Positioning System.

HOW DOES GPS WORK?

Developed by the Department of Defense in the 1970s, GPS is a gadget that takes readings from up to 24 satellites orbiting the earth every 12 hours. The satellites transmit continuous time and position data to receivers on the ground that enable troops to find their location, within 3 feet, anywhere in the world. And determine where an artillery shell or ICBM lands with equal accuracy. GPS units available for us ordinary outdoor types are accurate to within 100 yards or so. For accuracy, they should be used only in an open area, not under trees.

Not much larger than a mobile telephone, a handheld GPS unit reads signals from two or more satellites, then translates them into longitude and latitude. Look at your map. Put your finger where the latitude and longitude readings intersect and—that's where you are.

In addition to longitude and latitude, different GPS systems also provide a wide variety of other data. For example, a unit that takes three readings can instantly compute your altitude. The range of information available through GPS is increasing as fast as new systems are developed. They can, for instance, notify a motorist or a hiker which way to travel to reach a destination. Many rural police and fire departments use them in determining the source of a fire or a problem. Cars equipped with them tell the driver precisely how to reach a planned motel stop miles from the Interstate via back roads.

DO YOU NEED A GPS FOR BACKPACKING OR CANOEING?

One would be worthwhile for a hiker on vast stretches of open, flat terrain with few landmarks, or bushwhacking in unfamiliar territory. Canoeists might also find them useful to figure out where they are when paddling a river flowing in and out of lakes broken with small islands.

For backpackers and canoeists who follow familiar trails or rivers, a GPS receiver might be more fun than necessary. However, a GPS is never a substitute for a solid knowledge of how to use a map and compass.

HOW MUCH DOES A GPS COST?

Basic GPS units that can be carried in your pocket are widely popular for recreational boaters and hikers. A few years ago, these sold for about $2,000. Today, depending upon what different information you want, small, battery-powered units sell for $150 to $250. So prevalent are they with boaters that they are gradually replacing loran, the long-range navigation system that uses onshore beacons transmitting radio signals to establish locations.

TALKING GPS

Here are some common terms to talk today's GPS Talk:

LMK, or landmark: A fixed position used as a "waypoint" in navigation.

GOTO: This enables you to "go to" a saved landmark.

Route: Starting and ending landmarks.

Leg: A division of a route following landmarks.

HDG, or heading: The direction in which the GPS is moving.

BRG, or bearing: The direction you must go to reach a landmark.

XTE, or cross track error: The distance you are from the left or right of a planned path.

Map Reading 101

Required material: two U.S. Geological Survey contour maps—one large-scale 1:24,000 contour map that covers the general area where you live, and one small-scale 1:250,000 contour map that covers your entire region.

Class assignment: Using the distance scale on the bottom, mark the widths and heights of the map in miles.

Maps and compass in hand, go outside. Orient your large-scale map.

To do this, place your map on a flat surface well removed from any metal. At the bottom, or side, of the map is a cluster of three arrows. One is marked MN, another GN, and a third with a symbol for a star. Here is what each means:

MN—Magnetic North, or the direction your compass needle points. (MN has the same meaning on all maps.)

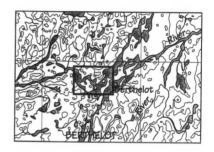

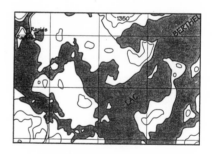

A "small-scale" 1:250,000 series Canadian map in which 1¼ inches on the map is equal to 5 miles, and a "large-scale" 1:50,000 series Canadian map in which 1¼ inches on the map equals 1 mile. In planning a lengthy trip, it's often a good idea to buy a small-scale map for a general view of the entire region, and a large-scale map for the great detail it reveals about the terrain you are hiking, biking, or paddling.

GN—Grid North, or the direction of the large square black lines that either are marked on the map, or are the north-south boundaries of the map. This is the north used by surveyors and the military.

Star symbol (*)—true north.

Align the MN arrow with your compass arrow. Now your map and the ground are in total sync.

Contour maps show the shape of the earth through flowing lines. A peak, for example, is where the lines form concentric circles that get smaller as the elevation increases. The summit is a circle. Lines far apart indicate flat or gently sloping land. Lines bunched together indicate a steep incline or cliff. Contour lines that form arrows indicate upstream, and Us a ridge or bluff.

Locate yourself on your large-scale map. You should have an instant awareness of the shape of the countryside around you and how easy it is to "read" the map as you look about.

Walk or drive through the neighborhood. Compare what you see on the map with the local territory. Notice how the hills in the distance are shown on the map. Check streams with how they appear on the map and on the ground. The shape of lakes. The roads.

Next, study your small-scale map. Compare the terrain features on it. Find the highest peak on the map. What is its elevation? Notice how the roads, rivers, lakes, and hills or mountains appear on the large-scale map compared with the way you see them on the small-scale map as well as with your eyes. Hey, reading maps isn't so difficult after all.

Term project: Afoot or afloat, travel three days over an area you've never been on before using your maps to guide you.

Grade yourself when you arrive safely home!

Marking Your Maps

On my trips to a new area I always buy enough large-scale maps to cover my entire trip, and one or more small-scale maps to cover the entire region in which we will be paddling or hiking.

Then I go over the small-scale map and mark both start and finish and lightly trace in waterproof color a line parallel to our route. I make a mark on a string for every 3 map miles. Using the string marks, I then mark small Xs on the color line parallel to the route for every 3 miles, and a series of circles every 12 miles, with the total mileage each one is from our starting point—for instance, (12) (24) (36)—and finally a very large X at the midway point. No matter how short or long the trip, midway means a fine bottle of wine with dinner.

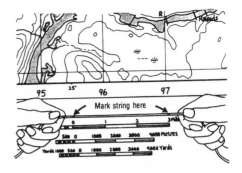

Whether on a trail or a river, premarking distances can be a great asset in knowing how far you have traveled in one day, or in a week. On my maps I make a mark, with distance from point of origin, every 3 miles.

While sitting at a desk in the comfort of my home, I mark on a map the azimuth we should be following if there is a sharp change in direction where we might become confused, such as which outlet from a lake we should be paddling. It's more comfortable than marking a map while kneeling in front of my tent.

Where to Buy Maps

If your local map dealer or outing goods store doesn't stock the essential contour maps you need, contact the U.S. Geological Survey, Map Sales, Box 25286, Federal Center, Denver CO 80225; tel 800-872-6277. For massive amounts of map information, check out the Web page: www.usgs.gov.

For Canadian maps contact the Surveys and Mapping Branch, Department of Energy, Mines and Resources, Ottawa, Canada.

Which Way Is North?

"Follow the Drinking Gourd."

In the shameful era of slavery in the South, the hope for freedom that burned endlessly in the souls of the slaves was to flee to Canada. Where was Canada? How did an ignorant human workhorse get there?

"Follow the Drinking Gourd."

And those who managed to escape and follow the intangible underground railway far enough toward the Drinking Gourd did cross into the freedom of our northern neighbor.

The Drinking Gourd, of course, is the Big Dipper. It has been pointing toward and circling the North Star for untold epochs, and giving all adventurous men since before the first vestiges of civilization a fixed point to judge direction.

When in doubt where north is after the stars sparkle at night, find the Big Dipper. The two stars forming the front of the dipper's bowl point directly toward bright Polaris, the North Star. It is about five times the distance between the two bowl stars to Polaris.

Determining north on sunny days is simple with a watch running on local time. Turn the face of the watch so the hour hand points directly to the sun. Halfway between the hour hand and 12 o'clock is south. So turn around. P.S. This isn't very effective before about 10 A.M. or after 4 P.M.

Here are a few techniques for roughly establishing direction. Moss tends to grow slightly heavier on the north side of trees. Since prevailing wind patterns are west to east, the tips of trees point east. Winter snows are heavier and last longer on the slopes facing north. The shadow cast by a tree is shortest at noon. The direction of the tree to the nadir of the shadow is north.

Three

Three.

Remember that number.

THREE! THREE! THREE!

Whether in mountain, or on desert, canoeing in the Northwest Territories, or on safari in Botswana, three means: HELP!

If you hear three blasts on a whistle, repeated; or three shotgun blasts, repeated in the same sequence; or see three smoky fires, or three Coast Guard–approved orange signal flags spread on the ground, someone needs help.

Caring for Your Maps

The sad, last words of a hiking chap
    were these: "I think I've lost my map."
Let all take heed from his grim plight:
    Ne'er let your map out of your sight.

No one intends to, of course. This is precisely why commercial map protectors sold at every outing and map store have a hole for slipping a protective string through. Instead of stuffing the topo document loosely into a pocket, tie the plastic container protecting the map to the pack, then stuff it into your pocket.

Commercial map holders are excellent for protecting maps from rain or damage. Maps can also be well protected by carrying them in Ziploc bags.

When wilderness canoeing, I tie my map to a thwart so I can keep a wary eye on it.

It is not necessary to carry a map fully spread out. Indeed, it is much more convenient to fold a topo map the same way as the highway maps that you have now in your glove compartment. Open it only to the area in which you are traveling.

Understanding Trail Markers

You may not actually need a contour map to find your way along thousands of miles of maintained cross-country hiking trails. They are well marked with special signs. For example, the 2,160-mile-long Appalachian Trail, which is hiked in part by some 4 million enthusiasts every year, is marked every 100 yards or so with the AT insignia: a white bar 2 inches wide and 6 inches long. These are painted by volunteer workers.

Appalachian Trail markers. Longitudinal white bars, such as the one at the top of the post, mark the entire trail from Maine to Georgia. Here's an example of how this 2-inch-wide, 6-inch-long bar keeps hikers safely on the trail in the wilderness.

Each trail has its own particular symbol and color—red circles, white circles, green circles, circles with a bar, squares, triangles, capital letters. Whatever.

All trails in the United States generally follow the AT pattern for denoting directions. Turns are marked by two trail markers, one slightly above and to the left or right of the lower one, meaning "trail here turns left or right." Occasionally the turn is augmented with the letter *L* or *R,* and an arrow. The end or beginning of trails usually is indicated by two trail markers side by side, or placed in a triangular pattern.

Marked and maintained trails inevitably mean that somewhere there is a map for that pathway over mountains and across swamps. If you will be on a strange trail, it's common sense to pick one up from whichever agency or outing club handles the trail maps in the area. Check the specific symbol and color of the markers on your trail.

You should not get lost, obviously, following a marked trail, though fog, storms, and snows may slightly impede your progress. However, since trail markers do not usually indicate the distance between points, a trail or contour map is your irreplaceable guide. Read the terrain on a contour map. Compare it with what you actually see. You should be able to locate yourself within 50 feet of where you are standing.

There is no confusion about which way to go when paddling a well-defined river. The confusion arises when you want to know precisely where, on a strange river or island-dotted lake, your canoe is floating. Do what all outdoor veterans do. Haul out the contour map. Read the terrain. Locate yourself. Within 50 feet of where you are paddling.

Stay Clear

If you're lost or in need of help, make camp on a trail, in a clearing, or at a wide-open space on a river shore.

Smoke 'Em

To keep a fire smoky, build it, and feed it, with freshly cut green branches. In a life-and-death emergency there is no conflict with low-impact camping.

The Mighty Compass

It's axiomatic that no one goes into the wilderness without a compass. The smarter traveler carries two, one tucked into his pocket, the other safely secured with the package of emergency equipment.

Magnetic compasses come in two basic styles: floating dial and needle. The floating dial has an arrow and an N printed on it. The dial always points north. The floating needle always points north, but the dial has to be rotated to coincide with north.

The most popular compass today is the orienteering model with a needle above a dial that can be rotated.

All better compasses have some means by which they can be set to give the user two norths: magnetic north and true or map north.

Of the two compasses I carry, one is an ancient World War II type with a floating dial. The other is the Suunto KB14, which has a floating dial, but I must actually look into the compass to see the dial and orient it toward my objective. This Suunto

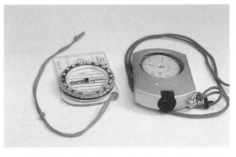

From left, a needle compass and a dial compass.

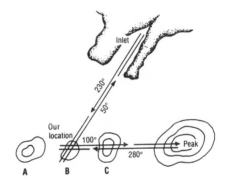

Using map and compass, here's a triangulation method of locating yourself if lost. First, orient the map so it is facing magnetic north. Second, locate a distinctive landmark you can find on the map, such as a high peak, and aim the compass toward it. Third, draw a back azimuth, or a line exactly 180 degrees opposite the sighting, toward you. Now you know you are somewhere on that line. Fourth, aim the compass toward another distinctive landmark. Fifth, draw a back azimuth from it. Where the two lines intersect is your exact location.

is remarkably effective. Handheld, it is accurate to within less than $\frac{1}{2}$ degree, a rate of accuracy far more important on ships than is necessary in a compass for the backpacker or canoeist.

8

The Campsite

In the light of a campfire, one sees a child's eyes glowing.
—Herb Gordon

 ## Establishing a Camp 101

Required material: Photographs of the last camp you set up.

Final will require you to actually walk through a potential campsite pointing to what will be located where, and a written list of at least 50 percent of the rules for setting up a camp.

SITE SELECTION AND PITCHING A TENT

- When possible, do not erect tents on grassy spots. This will protect the ground foliage. The thought of sleeping on hard, dry ground should be no cause for concern since, of course, each person carries a sleeping pad.
- Avoid camping at the bottom of a hill where rainwater could come bubbling down in a storm.
- Pitch tents well away and upwind from a campfire. Sparks carried downwind can burn holes in tents. It's a reasonably smart idea to pitch tents that are most affected by the wind, such as the older ∧-shaped tents, so that they face into, not crosswise to, the prevailing currents.
- If possible, pitch your tents under trees. The shade will keep a tent cooler by day. The branches will deflect rain. And the trees them-

selves will protect the tents from a tumultuous buffeting by strong winds.

Developing Campwise Kids

Before setting up camp let your children search for the appropriate area, and a specific site for their tent.

Encourage them to clear away chunks of wood, rocks, and twigs before putting down a plastic cloth a tad smaller than their tent, then pitch the tent on it. Plastic will protect the tent from damage and wet ground.

When the tent is taken down they must scatter ground debris over the site to make it appear that a tent was never erected there.

Give them the opportunity to pick out a place for a campfire, where to locate toilet facilities, and where and how to store food sacks during the day and at night.

Teach why it is necessary to pack out garbage that cannot be properly disposed of in camp.

When the campfire burns low, join hands, sing one last song, "Taps":

"Day is done, gone the sun, from the lake, from the hills, from the sky. All is well. Safely rest. God is nigh."

- Select the most level place possible. If there is even a slight slope, wary sleepers have a gravitational habit of sliding inch by inch toward the low end of the tent.

LOW-IMPACT CAMPING TIPS

- When tents are taken down, scatter ground detritus where the tents stood, just as you cover the site where you made a fire.
- In pristine sites, try not to follow the same path when walking down to the river for water so as not to create a trail in the grasses. Wilderness areas are not playgrounds for either the big or little. Destructive field games such as tossing Frisbees, playing catch, or a rousing round of touch football will tear delicate turf to pieces.
- If there are toilet facilities, use them. If not, go at least 200 feet from the nearest water, dig a cat hole, and bury feces and toilet paper under a few inches of dirt.
- It will also help keep a wilderness site clean to dig a small hole far from the kitchen area and dump greasy kitchen water into it.
- Locate garbage facilities 100 feet from tents.
- Locate food storage at least 50 feet from tents.

NO TOILET PAPER?

An extremist concept among some ultraprotectionists is that campers use stones or leaves in the summer, or snowballs in the winter, as a substitute for toilet paper. They argue that toilet paper may not disintegrate quickly, and that it can be dug up by animals. This approach left Dr. Wade Johnson aghast. His warnings were vehement and simple: The anus could become dangerously infected from dirty stones or leaves, or smeared with painful toxin by anyone who inadvertently grabs up poison ivy or poison sumac. As for snowballs, his medical comment was: "Brrrrrrr!" He also pointed out that anal/oral contact, readily possible by those who use stones or leaves, is the major cause of giardiasis among backpackers.

STRICTLY FOR WOMEN

No woman is so totally regular in her menstrual cycle that it cannot be upset during vigorous outdoor activity. It may not happen, but the experienced woman goes prepared. One key piece of advice a friend told me (she in turn had learned it from the woman who was leading her one-week backpacking trip) was to carry several pads in addition to her tampons. In a sudden emergency, these can be applied discreetly almost anywhere, at any hour. Tampons cannot be put into use quite so tactfully.

Used sanitary supplies should never be buried. They will be dug up almost as soon as they are covered with dirt. It is recommended that women carry a personal supply of small resealable plastic bags to put them in until they can be disposed of in a camp garbage bag, or burned.

Love in the Wilderness

As discussed in chapter 3, single-person sleeping bags come in three basic shapes: mummy, semi-mummy, and rectangular. Regardless of shape, some bags also can be purchased that zip together to make a double bag. To avoid the irritation of discovering on location that two bags cannot be united, unfamiliar bags should be pretested when possible.

Amorous couples should be aware that at night, tents with interior illumination can project vivid shadows of occupant activities. It also is necessary to stress that while copulating couples are isolated from their nearby wilderness friends by darkness and the tent itself, tent fabric is not sound resistant.

The Wood Fire versus Camp Stove Debate

Building a fire for wilderness cooking is becoming an increasingly hot issue between those who advocate camp stoves only and those who cook over a grill.

The stove-only purists argue that wood fires are destructive of woodlands and unnecessarily soil the environment: Campsites are covered with fire rings and littered with burned chunks of wood and charcoal.

Wood fire advocates argue, on the other hand, that wood is a renewable resource. Campers are still building fires in the same woods where their great-grandparents camped a century ago. The oil burned in camp stoves is a nonrenewable resource. Once gone, forever gone. And, they add, what the stove-only campers don't see is the destruction of the environment where oil rigs pump night and day, and the tremendous energy cost of moving oil from the fields and converting it into useful fuel.

Well, the bottom line is that there is room for campfire cooks *and* camp stove chefs. Those who light the kindling must do so with respect for the environment. Those who light the stoves have got to stop being smug about how "clean" stoves are and consider the total cost of burning a nonrenewable resource.

In addition, every campfire enthusiast should carry a camp stove. There are times when fires are prohibited because of forest fire danger, and others when it is impossible to build a cooking fire—because of wild weather, for instance, or while camping in areas where there is no wood. At such times a fine camp stove is a meal-cooking blessing.

Building Campfires

MAKE A LOW IMPACT

For wilderness travelers who cook with fires, observe the laws of low-impact camping:

1. Build no fire larger than necessary. It is wasteful to stoke up a roaring fire only to heat water for coffee.
2. Build a fire only when it can be put into service, not an hour before you need its flickering flame for dinner.

3. Build an efficient fire to conserve fuel.
4. Roaring campfires belong to yesterday. If you build a campfire at night, keep it small. Enjoy, do not destroy.

FOUR BASIC STYLES OF CAMPFIRES

In a sense, ther are only four basic styles of campfires—the hunter, trapper, trench, and Indian. Here is how each is built:

Hunter: The original hunter fire built in generations long gone by hunters and anglers consisted of two freshly cut logs, about 6 feet long and 1 foot thick. These were placed in a V, a few inches apart at the end facing the prevailing breeze, and 10 to 15 inches apart at the other. The fire was built between the logs at a width where the logs could support cooking pots and pans.

The logs have now been replaced by two parallel walls of stone about 1 foot high and only wide enough to support the grills. The walls face the prevailing breeze. If the breeze is too strong, a stone or slab of wood can be placed at the "front" to keep the wind from blowing the heat away. Some campers also place a large stone at the "back" of the two walls to form a "chimney," which gives additional heat to pots on the back end of the fire.

Trench: This is merely a fire built in a pit about 2 feet long and 10 inches deep, and only wide enough to support the grills. The fire trench should slope at one end so wood can be fed into the flame.

Indian: A favorite with Indians was a fire built of several long branches placed like the spokes of a wheel. The fire was built where the poles met. As they burned down, the poles were simply pushed into the hub.

Trapper: This combination fireplace and cooking fire was popular with the same hunters and anglers who built the original hunter fire when they expected to be in the same place for at least several days. It consisted of a back wall 5 or 6 feet high made of rocks or green logs a foot thick. The wall was slanted slightly backward. The fire built in front of the back wall was used for cooking, or kept burning through the night to reflect heat into a lean-to.

WHICH FIRES ARE BEST FOR COOKING?

The hunter and trench fires are the most efficient for cooking. Their walls reflect the heat upward.

Although widely popular, the most wasteful of firewood is an open fire with a commercial grill that sits on four foldaway legs. Every wisp of breeze blows heat from the pots and pans.

BUILD IT DOWNWIND

It's axiomatic that a campfire is always built downwind from the tents. It is helpful when setting up a campsite if the wind is from the prevailing direction. To determine this, look at the very tips of the tops of the trees. The tips always point in the prevailing direction of the wind. If the late-afternoon breeze is from an off direction when you are setting up camp, build your fire so that when the breezes return to their usual direction your tents still will be upwind from a fire site and safe from flying sparks.

CHOOSING THE BEST WOODS FOR CAMPFIRES

Gone are the days when . . . when campers scouted the woods for the appropriate tree to chop down for the campfire. Now fires, if they are built, are made only out of fallen branches without worrying about what kind of tree shed them. If you did have the option of cutting any wood you wanted, here is Kephart's advice on which wood to use in camp, and why:

> Best of all is hickory, green or dry. It makes a hot fire but lasts a long time, burning down to a bed of hard coals that keep up an even, generous heat for hours. . . . Following hickory in fuel value are the chestnut oak, overcup, post, and basket oaks, pecan, the hornbeams (ironwood), and dogwood. The latter burns finally to a beautiful white ash that is characteristic; applewood does the same.

> All of the birches are good fuel, ranking in about this order: black, yellow, red, paper, and white. Sugar maple's the favorite fuel of our old-time hunters and surveyors, but it is too valuable a tree, nowadays, to be cast into fire.

> Locust is a good, lasting fuel; it is easy to cut, and, when green, splits fairly well. Mulberry has similar qualities. The

best of the oaks for fuel, especially when green, is white oak.

Most of the softwoods are good only for kindling, or for quick cooking fires. The best green softwoods for fuel are white birch, paper birch, soft maple, cottonwood, and quaking aspen. For a cooking fire that will burn quickly to coals, without smoke, the bark of dead hemlock, hickory, pine, or sugar maple cannot be excelled.

CLEAN IT UP!

You built it. You cooked on it. You enjoyed its warming flames at night. When you pack up to move on, clean up. Scatter blackened rocks from a temporary fire ring, and place them facedown. Cover the trench fire with the dirt you saved. Be a low-impact camper even if you pitched your tents in a well-used camping area.

Cooking with Charcoal

Campers who carry a charcoal broiler know that charcoal is a fine substitute for the unique flavor that only the live coals from a campfire give to the foods on the grill.

But . . . to actually achieve this delicious gourmet touch, use only pure hardwood charcoal chunks, the same charcoal that elegant restaurants use when they broil food. Unfortunately, few stores carry the pure charcoal pieces; instead, they sell consumers "charcoal briquettes," which

A Better Bellow

There are three reasons why an Indian did not grab: 1. a frying pan, 2. a pot lid, or 3. his hat to fan a stubborn fire into a sparkling blaze. He did not possess any of them.

Nor did he squat down and puff like hell because, as even modern, sophisticated, well-equipped campers who sleep in sleek tents instead of tepees know, that isn't much better than fanning with pots, pans, and hats.

What he used to fire up a dismal flicker was a mouth bellow.

Never heard of a mouth bellow? An Indian would use a hollow reed about 3 feet long and, placing one end close to the piteous sparks, blow vigorously through it to bring the sickly blaze swiftly to life.

Try it yourself. You don't need to search for a reed. Use a 3-foot-long $\frac{1}{4}$- or $\frac{3}{8}$-inch rubber or plastic tube. It will work as fast and efficiently as a reed.

When not in use, keep it in your camp utility bag or your backpack. It will always be there when your fire needs a friendly puff.

are crushed charcoal of any wood, treated with oil, then compressed into briquettes.

To rid the briquettes of their oils, they must be burned until they are coated with ash. A few pieces of well-soaked shredded hardwood added to briquettes will impart some of that impossible-to-duplicate smoke flavoring.

Charcoal briquettes are widely available, but only a few stores stock pure hardwood charcoal. Some will order it on request. Many lumberyards carry 10- and 20-pound sacks of hardwood charcoal from Canada, or know lumberyards that do. Or try the Yellow Pages.

The Indispensable Camp Stove

Given the problems and regulations and weather for those who wander the barren deserts and forested mountains of our great outdoor regions, whether afoot or afloat, on bike or horseback, a camp stove is essential. Even the most determined fire-only camper will agree to this.

Consider:

1. A fire warden "bear" sign at the road that goes into the forest warns: OPEN FIRES NOT PERMITTED.
2. After two days and nights of rain, the third morning dawns in a driving snowstorm.
3. The desert is ablaze at the time of the year you visit—with great fields of flowers. No trees.
4. Without belaboring the obvious, camp stoves are also what make it possible to eat hot meals in the challenge of backpacking far above timberline. There are no helicopter deliveries of order-in hot meals at Camp Three on the flanks of Mount Everest.
5. Where camping is possible only on wood platforms in the Everglades, cooking is not—unless you have your camp stove.

If there isn't one in your gear today, buy one!

STOVE STYLES

The most significant difference among camp stoves is that some burn gasoline or other liquid fuel such as kerosene or alcohol, and others burn butane, propane, or a combination of gases. Backpackers, high-altitude climbers, and canoeists tend to favor the gasoline fuel stoves. They burn hotter than the butane/propane stoves and, unlike butane/propane stoves, can be used in freezing temperatures.

There is no genuine problem in running out of fuel when using gasoline. Fill the tank before starting to cook. The only way to determine when the propane/ butane canister will sigh and die is either to keep careful track of

The double-burner camp stove at the end of the table is popular with car campers. These usually burn propane or butane. They are too heavy for long-distance canoeing or backpacking.

the length of time a canister has been used, or to watch the flame go out. Even in the middle of cooking a superb chicken cacciatore.

The butane/propane stove is simple to use. Screw the burner unit to the top of the gas canister. Light a match. Start cooking.

Gasoline stoves take a bit longer to heat up.

SELECTING THE RIGHT STOVE FOR YOUR WILDERNESS TRAVEL

Here is some descriptive information about several of the more widely used stoves. On average, all of them will boil a quart of water at room temperature in four to six minutes.

Propane/Butane: Not recommended for cold-weather or winter camping.

- Camping Gas Turbo 270 HP; the gas canisters are widely available around the world. Weight about 10 ounces without canister.
- Peak 1 Micro Butane; uses Peak 1 3100 canister. A small unit best suited for singles or couples. Weight with canister 12.2 ounces.

A couple of pan lids, or metal plates, can vastly improve the efficiency of a small camp stove: Use them to block the wayward breezes.

- MSR Rapid Fire; weight about 12 ounces without canister; uses ISO/Butane.
- Coleman two-burner, propane; weight about 9 ounces without canister. Best for family car campers.

Gasoline: Recommended for use in any season.

- Optimus 111; weight 54 ounces, includes gas tank and metal cover. Burns leaded and unleaded gasoline and kerosene; this is a tough workhorse of the outdoor fraternity.
- Optimus 123; weight 13 ounces, including tank. Burns only white gasoline. Excellent for small groups.
- Optimus SR; weight 13 ounces, including tank. Burns only white gasoline. One of the smallest stoves on the market; useful when weight and/or size is critical.
- MSR X/GK; weight about 16 ounces without canister; burns white, leaded, or unleaded gasoline; kerosene, diesel fuel, and Stoddard Solvent No. 1. Outstanding when heading for primitive country where fuel can be a major problem.
- MSR Whisperlite; weight about 14 ounces without canister; burns only white gas. Popular with high mountaineers.
- On all my group outdoor trips, whether canoeing or backpacking, we carry one or two Optimus 111Bs; weight about 50 ounces. It burns only white gasoline.

My first recommendation in shopping for portable camp stoves is to avoid the two-burner units. If you need two stoves for a large group, buy two individual units. Each stove can be placed wherever the cook wants it. This can be important in a wilderness camp where there is no convenient table on which to place a double burner.

HOW MUCH DO CAMP STOVES COST?

Butane/propane style stoves (excluding the cost of fuel canisters): small, three season, from $25 to $45; large, four season, $50 to $100. Gasoline, all season, small, $75 plus; large, $125 plus.

CAMP STOVE MAINTENANCE

Whether gasoline or propane/butane, all stoves must be carefully maintained and cleaned regularly. With proper care, your daughter will take that new stove with her when she goes wilderness trekking 20 years from now.

Home–Baked Goodness on the Trail

Today's campers who sigh for freshly baked bread, or pies bursting with handfuls of delicious berries plucked from bushes growing behind the tent, can make wondrous use of portable "reflector" ovens, available at all sporting goods stores. Placed in front of the bright flames of the campfire, heat is reflected from an angled overhead sheet of shiny aluminum onto a flat sheet of metal on which the cakes and pies are placed.

Such ovens have been around for centuries. Made out of heavy metal, they were once placed in front of fireplaces replete with chains and braces for holding iron kettles and pans for all cooking.

The Traditional Earthen Oven

Far into an eon of yesterdays, in the dim years before humankind had learned to make iron, busy housewives were baking breads and roasting meats. What they used was something as simple as an earthen oven.

In fact, that same style of oven is in use in some remote regions of the world even today—and by those who enjoy the challenge of not only digging one, but actually cooking in it.

Here is a description of what was called the "clay oven," written by Horace Kephart nearly a century ago:

> Find a clay bank or steep knoll near by. Dig down the bank to a vertical front. Back from this front, about 4 feet, drive a 4 or 5 inch stake down to what will be the bottom level of the oven. Draw the stake out, thus leaving a hole for the

The Gasoline Dilemma

Carrying gasoline can be a problem whether traveling by train or plane in the United States or abroad. As we boarded a train once in Canada, a conductor spied us openly carrying a gallon can of gasoline for our stoves. "No way," he waved. "Not on this train." We handed our gasoline to a startled local workman, and climbed aboard. When the train made a 10-minute stop at a village, one of us, fearful we might not be able to buy gasoline at the remote water-tank stop where we would disembark, leaped off the train, streaked for a local store near the depot, bought a gallon, hid it under his coat, and returned to the train. We all smiled.

flue. Now from the bottom of the face, dig a horizontal hole back to the flue, keeping the entrance as small as you can, but enlarging the interior and arching its top. When the oven is finished, wet this whole interior, smooth it, and build a small fire in the oven to gradually dry and harden it.

To bake in such an oven: build a good fire in it of split hardwood sticks, and keep it burning hard for an hour or two; then rake out the embers, lay your dough on broad green leaves (basswood, from choice) or on the naked floor, and close both the door and the flue with flat stones or bark.

Hole–in–the–Ground Cookery

Only three elements are necessary to steam-bake in camp: a strong back, a good shovel, and something to cook.

One method popular with anglers and hunters in the days when they drove to camp in a light wagon hauled by a couple of horses was, essentially, a seashore clambake.

Known then as a "Chinook bake," it began with a large fire covered with round, moderate-sized stones. While the stones were heating, a hole was dug in the ground next to the fire. Once the stones were white hot, they were shoveled into the hole, leveled, and thickly covered with wet leaves, grass, or even small branches. The meat—which could be whatever was brought along, or freshly shot, skinned, and appropriately butchered—and potatoes were tossed in and covered with another heavy layer of leaves, then with a layer of dirt. A hole was bored through the dirt, water poured in, and the hole promptly covered, letting the food steam until, either by experience or guesswork, it was properly cooked.

Necessity: The Mother of Invention

CAMP BROOM

Need a broom to keep your camp clean? First, gather a handful or two of hemlock twigs, about 8 to 10 inches long. Then find a nice length of deadwood for the handle. Tie the twigs firmly with twine or vines to the handle. Now chop off the ends of the twigs evenly. There, in 10 minutes, is a fine little broom to clean up around the fire and keep the camp neat.

Follow the same procedure for a whisk broom to clean sand and junk out of your tent. Sooner or later you'll hear: "Hey, that's neat. Could I borrow it?"

Put together your own camp broom. Chop a half-dozen or so twig tips into 12-inch lengths. Then, using a spare shoelace or piece of cord, tie them to a 3-foot branch.

CAMP SHOVEL

Whether you forgot a trowel or small shovel to dig a cat hole or for other digging purposes, or you left it at home to keep your pack a few ounces lighter, not to worry. Find yourself a stick 2 inches in diameter, preferably beech or hickory, and about 18 inches long. Next, rotate one end in the fire until it is well charred. Do not let it catch fire. The charred wood will be much stronger than the fresh wood.

When cool, shave the charred end, on one side only, until it is sloping flat. Now—dig with it. Or stir up the fire.

POT LIFTER

Almost any sturdy stick 3 or 4 feet long will make a fine pot lifter if it has a knob or twig 2 or 3 inches long. Cut the stick so the knob or twig is at its bottom end.

As you will see, the camp broom really works. So clean up!

Smooth off all the other branches. This works, of course, only with pots with a single handle.

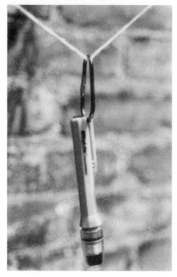

Every tent has, or should have, a cord permanently tied across the top. Now it's simple to hang a one-cell mini light to the cord and leave it there—even when you pack up and head for home. It's your fancy ceiling light. Put aside your camp flashlight for more important purposes.

CAMPFIRE TONGS

Every kitchen area needs a set of tongs. Start off with a green stick of beech or hickory, at least an inch thick, and 2 or 3 feet long. Shave a 3-inch-long segment off one side of the center until it is ½ inch thick.

Next, hold the shaved center over hot embers until you can bend the stick freely. Bring the ends of the stick together, whittling the tips flat so they fit smoothly. Then cut light checks across the inside so the tongs have a good grip.

If the two sides of the tongs do not hold reasonably parallel after the stick cools, tie them to the correct position with a piece of vine or sturdy string.

PROTECTING A LANTERN

To protect a camp lantern against damage when carrying it in a canoe, wrap it in a piece of an old closed-cell ground pad lying in the basement. No old pad in the basement? Peel a large chunk of bark off a birch tree and tie it carefully around the lantern. Peel off only outer bark, without damaging the cambium layer.

CANOE TABLE

A canoe isn't exactly a camp gadget, but it's handy to have one around for a number of onshore uses.

First—convert a canoe into a table.

Roll the canoe upside down. Use sturdy stones or chunks of wood to wedge the bow and stern decks or gunwales so the canoe does not wobble. Now enjoy the pleasure of using the upended bottom of the canoe as a work or serving table.

If you're cooking with an outdoor stove, it's an accepted practice to place the stove on top of the canoe. However, in doing this, remember that even the most efficient stove can have problems. An over-heated gasoline stove could damage the canoe material itself. And, of course, never use a canoe table as a chopping block or cutting board.

Second—use the canoe for overnight storage. Put kindling, camp gear, and equipment under the overturned canoe at night to protect it from dew or rain.

Lost your spoon? Make one out of a mussel shell. Tuck it into a cracked stick and hold it there with a couple of plastic ties. Also note well that the Sierra Cup has the initials of its proud and jealous owner clearly marked on it in nail polish. Hey, don't touch.

FORKS AND SPOONS

Lost your fork? Not to worry. Shave a pair of twigs about the size of chopsticks smooth. Now use them as chopsticks.

Oh, your problem is a spoon that disappeared a couple of days ago? Find yourself a large freshwater mussel shell. Cut a thin slice lengthwise into the end of a small stick. Wedge the shell into the slice and put your new spoon to work.

Bearproofing Your Campsite

In the wilderness, animals range from pests to perilous.

The porcupine is on the annoying edge of the spectrum. Porcupines gnaw at anything containing salt. They will chew on a well-used paddle handle permeated with salt from perspiration, as well as find gourmet delight in shoelaces.

Packrats will drag small items, a key chain or a coin, from an untended tent or an open shelter. Raccoons may be a delight to watch if they come sauntering into your camp. They also are clever at getting into open bags containing anything from garbage to edibles.

In the danger zone are bears. Grizzlies, whose Latin name is, appropriately, *Ursus horribilis,* are the most fearsome backpackers and campers are likely to meet. Smaller black and brown bears, however, are the most common.

Being attacked by a wild animal is an occurrence so rare that it will merit attention on TV news programs that otherwise are chock-a-block with every cruddy local crime story in the area.

The vast bulk of stories, legends, and reports about animals savagely attacking humans without cause are, in a single word: bunk.

Humans have feared wolves for centuries. However, wolves do not leap out of nowhere to attack humans. Both grizzly and Alaskan bears are feared because of their reputation for charging humans without provocation. Don't believe it.

Yes, humans have been badly mauled and killed by animals, but careful investigations into these incidents have revealed that they generally were triggered by human errors, such as keeping food beside or in a tent, or in a sleeping bag, or inadvertently surprising a dangerous animal in its own wooded hideaway.

Male grizzlies usually weigh in at over 350 pounds; the female, 250 pounds. Adults can stand 6 feet tall on their hind legs. Fortunately for the outdoor fraternity, their habitat is largely confined to the northern Rockies, Alaska, and the remote northwestern Canadian wilderness. Wilderness grizzlies are rarely known to prowl through a tent site in a seldom-used area in search of food. They prefer the major camping areas where scraps and foolish campers abound.

PROTECTING FOOD

If a bear strolls into your camp sniffing for a meal, he wants it wherever it is. If you catch sight of him, make a disturbance—a flashlight at night, a whistle, hollering, banging two lids, throwing stocks or stones—from a distance. This almost—almost—always frightens him off. If it doesn't, it is the better part of valor to make a hasty retreat.

Beware the Bear Piñata: A long-practiced technique that supposedly safeguards your next dinner in bear country is to hang food sacks. One method is to string a line between two trees, with the food sacks hung in the middle and at least 15 feet from the ground and 10 feet from the nearest branch. Another is to sling a line from a branch well away from the trunk and hang the food sacks on it.

Does hanging food really foil bears seeking a snack? Or is the food safe only when no hungry bears come around? Steve Thompson, the wildlife biologist at Yosemite

National Park, California, says basically the food is perfectly safe—only when no bears come nosing around.

Thompson says "Bears have elaborate schemes for getting food. One time-honored precaution, hanging bags of food from a rope high in a tree, is now seen as useless. Local residents call the food bags 'bear piñatas.'

"The bears chew off the rope that has been attached elsewhere, or chew off the branch that is supporting the bag. If the limbs are small, they'll send the cubs out. If that doesn't work, they'll just climb above the bags, launch themselves out of the tree, and grab the bags on the way down."

Bear-Resistant Food Storage Strategies: Today, Thompson advises worried backpackers to carry food in tough, bear-resistant canisters. These are PVC tubes 8 inches in diameter with a secure lid. They are intentionally large so that bears cannot carry them off in their mouths. They are bulky for backpackers but pose no particular problem for canoeists or car campers.

Food also can be stored in pots with tight lids, or the waterproof packs used by canoeists and kayakers, then put into a streambed or the edge of a lake and held underwater, if necessary, by rocks. The theory: If animals cannot smell the food, they won't look for it.

Unopened commercial packages of food are usually immune from attack.

Of course all food should be stored at least 50 feet from the tents, no matter what system you use.

Scare 'Em: If hanging food sacks is useless and you don't have PVC canisters, what else can be done to protect your precious edibles?

In a half century of camping, backpacking, canoeing, and rock climbing from western mountains to the Alps, I've always used the "scare 'em with noise" system. Simple:

At night, the food sacks are stacked in a single pile on top of an upside-down canoe or a camp table—well away from the tents—and covered with a poncho. Then all the pots and pans are stacked loosely on top of the poncho. The theory is that if an animal comes nosing around, she'll knock the pots and pans off. The noise will frighten her and she'll run away—empty mouthed.

Only twice, in all those years of wonderful memory, did I ever have a "problem" with bears.

We were backpacking in Idaho's Sawtooth Mountains—big-bear country. I was awakened one chilly predawn by the clatter of the pots and pans and peered out my tent to see a dark rump padding swiftly off—empty mouthed. However, there was another early dawn, canoeing in the northwestern Quebec wilderness, when I again heard clatter and banging. I peaked out the tent to catch sight of a bear running off, but dragging a food sack with him.

When the camp was awake I assembled our group and told them what happened. We could see traces in the dust on the ground where the bear had dragged the pack. With all the skill of well-trained hunting dogs, we followed the tracks and drags and found the bag about 100 yards into the woods. The bear had ripped it open, eaten a few goodies, then departed, leaving the majority of food for us to serve up another day.

Avoiding Problems with Animals 101

Required material: None.

While the likelihood of an attack by a wild animal is possible, the chances are slim if you follow a few rules. For this class you are required to memorize five basic rules. These will be thoroughly discussed. We have arranged an overnight visit to a wilderness campsite. You will submit notes on what you have observed for a final.

One: You are a guest in the animal's territorial home. Taken by surprise on a trail or near her den, an animal may attack. When hiking along a seldom-traveled trail, or packing canoes across a remote portage, make noise. Sing. Blow a whistle. Yell to each other. Animals usually edge quickly away from tumult and shouting.

Two: Keep the camp clean. No food of any kind in any tent at any time. No garbage stacked by a tent. No scraps scattered in the camp. Haul the garbage sack 100 feet into the woods at night. Clean fish 200 feet away from the campsite.

Three: If you see a baby animal apparently alone, never approach him or come between the animal and his mother. Her reaction can be swift and violent.

Four: In an area popular with campers, animals may wander in looking for tidbits. Do not attempt to attract any "friendly" animal by holding out a scrap or tossing food. He could tear away a few of your fingers snapping for the food or attack you while hunting for more.

Five: Do not approach a large standing or feeding animal, such as a bear, moose, or elk, so you can get a close up with your Instamatic. Animals are not impressed by your desire to capture them on film and may attack if they feel threatened. Use a telephoto lens. It's safer.

Camp Creeps

As though it isn't enough to worry about bears stealing your food packs, or being attacked by a rutting moose, or stepping on a hostile rattlesnake, heading into the wilds has increasingly become a problem at the more popular campsites with such human creeps as camp thieves and car robbers.

Herewith some advice offered by a security officer at a national forest campground in Idaho.

Never ever leave any valuables in a car where they can be seen, or even locked in a trunk in a remote area. Thieves are well known for smashing car windows or ripping open trunks with crowbars. If you are doubtful about leaving valuables in your car while climbing a mountain to admire the scenery, consider putting them in a waterproof bag and hiding it in the woods.

An antitheft device on the steering wheel will help prevent car thieves who may be prowling about outdoor camps from stealing your transportation home.

Be cautious about talking with casual strangers in a camp area who would like to find out where you are going and how long you will be gone.

Even though you have an excellent built-in warning signal to frighten thieves in a city, a car's alarm wailing away at a lonely wilderness site could be meaningless except to frighten squirrels and hungry bears. It probably won't stop the thieving hand.

The security officer recommended that every car have a clearly visible lock on the steering wheel, such as the Club, which he considered a major deterrent, because few camp thieves carry tools to break them loose.

Losing car keys can be a miserable experience 30 miles from the nearest telephone. Consider hiding a key somewhere inside a bumper, or shoving it under a wheel as though you had driven on top of it.

Winter Camping

One of the dividends of winter camping is that camp areas are virtually, or totally, empty of other campers. No noisy crowd in the next site, boomboxes shattering the night. Set up your tents wherever you want.

Traveling is easy. Via snowmobile for the car camping family. Not quite so simple for the pure of heart, although you can travel via cross-country skis on virgin snow, or clomp along on snowshoes. The latter now range from light, aluminum frames with synthetic "soles" to traditional snowshoes of leather strips woven onto wooden frames. Snowshoes are readily available for rent at many outdoor equipment stores and ski shops. But to enjoy an exhilarating weekend when you see your breath every time you exhale, you must go fully prepared, from equipment to clothing to food. And you must know the warning signs of problems, and how to treat them.

WHAT KIND OF TENT WILL YOU NEED?

For overnighting, a four-season tent is in the classification of mandatory. All of the better tent manufacturers specifically identify their four-seasoners. Though they may not look much different from any tent, the fabric is stronger and slightly heavier than in summer tents. The fly must completely cover the tent itself and should provide a protected space under which wet and snowy gear can be stuffed without cluttering the sleeping quarters. On the trail, set up tents in a defilade to avoid the chill of winter wind.

FUELING THE BODY'S FURNACE WITH FOOD

The foundation for keeping warm in the chill of winter begins with your own body furnace. Turn up the heat it produces with calories, lots of fat and juicy calories. Winter activists burn up calories at an astounding rate. To maintain comfort on an icy trail by following a low-calorie, hold-down-the-fat-and-avoid-the-salt diet is precisely wrong. *Add* calories—especially fats, the most concentrated form of food energy. Long after your body has digested carbohydrates and sugars for quick energy, the fat will still be providing fuel for warmth. Fat has almost twice the calories per gram of any other nutrient. At least one-third of your calories should come from fats.

Chewing chunks of blubber with, or between, meals is a winter-survival technique the Inuit have practiced for centuries. Mountaineers who head for the highest peaks, where they cross glaciers on their way to the summit, often carry sticks of sausage to chew on during the day to stoke the body's fuel level.

Protein is fuel for tissue growth and critical for all body processes. The body doesn't burn stored protein for energy until it burns up fat reserves. Proteins should make up from 10 to 20 percent of your daily calories.

Vegetarians reluctant to turn to fat-rich meats still can slather on the butter, eat cheese and nuts, and drink whole milk. And all of us can gulp down those rich, tasty desserts we only fantasize about at home.

KEEPING HYDRATED

Even on the coldest days, the body sweats. At high altitudes, dry air swiftly removes body moisture via respiration. Water is a temperature regulator, so the fluid must be replaced—if for no other reason than to increase body comfort.

All caffeinated fluids, including coffee, tea, and colas, as well as drinks with alcohol, are diuretics, speeding the loss of body fluid.

Advocates of leave-out-the-salt must be aware that, since salt helps the body retain fluid, it's important to return to normal salt usage.

A bowl of warm soup heated over a portable camp stove at lunch is a fine way to add liquid and fuel. Every camp dinner should begin with soup.

LAYERING FOR WARMTH

Dress in layers. The first layer is your body's own natural oil. This invisible layer helps the cells retain moisture and the body stay warmer. Forget the silliness of taking a bath or shower or wiping the body oils off with a damp cloth.

Next, underwear. Polypropylene fabrics are excellent, wicking moisture from the body, but holding in the heat. On particularly icy days, some outdoor types wear light silk underwear next to the skin, then polypro long johns. *Warning:* Cheap "winter" underwear made of cotton is an invitation to disaster, no matter how fancy the weave.

Two light garments are better at holding in warmth than one heavy garment. On days when you get too warm, one layer can be stuffed into your pack. So start with a warm turtleneck sweater, then add a down-filled or fleece vest.

Next, pants and coat. Ski clothing is super, especially if made with a water-resistant outer layer that permits body moisture to escape but prevents rain from entering. Old water-resistant fabrics can lose their water resistance with time. Try treating them with a water-repellent spray, such as Scotch-Guard.

Bib-style pants are the warmest. If you wear pants held up with a belt, toss away the belt and use sturdy suspenders.

Occasionally, snowflakes fall as rain. If your clothing is not 100 percent rainproof, carry a large plastic garbage bag. To wear it, turn the bag upside down and cut a hole in the bottom only big enough to slide your head through, and cut armholes on the sides. So, let 'er rain. When the rain ends, roll up the bag and stuff it into a pocket.

Wear only top-quality socks made of either wool or polypro fabrics. They should be moderately snug, but never tight. Tight socks restrict the flow of blood to the feet, compounding the problem of icy tootsies. If you suffer sweaty feet, rub them down with an antiperspirant before putting on your socks.

Since up to 50 percent of body heat is lost through the head, wear only a truly warm water-resistant cap that can be pulled down to cover the ears and forehead. On the coldest days, add a neck gaiter. When the wind blows, pull it up to cover your face.

For snowy trails, nothing less than ankle-high boots with an inner lining that wicks away moisture. For cross-country skiers, especially, consider adding ankle gaiters, which are helpful in keeping snow and ice from getting inside your boots.

For wear around camp take a look at the new lightweight waterproof boots that fit over your shoes. They come in two lengths: 9 inches and 15 inches. For trail hiking, another new product, Ice Treds, is a rubber with four steel spikes for extra traction. A pair slips easily over regular shoes or boots.

This snowshoeing couple trekking along the trails at Idaho's fabled Sun Valley resort must know that up to 50 percent of body heat is lost through the head. Notice they're wearing headgear that can be pulled down to cover the ears and forehead. On colder days, add a neck gaiter.

Oh, there's another item for the cold camping days: Bring along a half dozen, or more, of those little plastic bags filled with chemicals that become warm when they are massaged.

THE NIPPY NOSE AND FROSTBITTEN TOES

The temperature, not the altitude, of where you go snowshoeing or hiking, is the cause of "frostnip" or the more dangerous "frostbite." Both usually occur without any sense of pain. The first sign of trouble is white skin, especially around the face and ears. The wise will check each other occasionally for the telltale warnings.

Treat frostnip by rewarming the skin with a warm hand, or by blowing on it gently; then cover the exposed skin and head off to a warm area. When the skin is warmed, it may itch, but there will be no permanent damage.

In frostbite, a deeper layer of skin actually freezes into ice crystals. The frozen skin is white and hard. It's imperative that the victim of frostbite get medical treatment as swiftly as possible. Never rub or massage frozen skin, since this may tear the affected cells, causing permanent damage. Protect the skin by covering it with a cloth—never any ointment or heat—until proper medical help can be obtained.

Even under proper treatment, frostbitten skin tissues swell. The pain is brutal. The affected skin may be covered with blood-filled blisters, which can result in gangrene.

Hypothermia can occur under any weather conditions. Review how to treat it in chapter 6.

 # Checking Out of the Wilderness Motel

DON'T TRASH MOTHER NATURE

Exactly what is garbage? To some—everything that came in with you that you didn't eat. Everything. Stuff it all into plastic garbage bags and take it out. Leave nothing, as the old saying has it, not even footprints.

However, barring this extreme approach, here are some things careful and courteous campers should always take into consideration:

In well-used areas, bury nothing. No cans. No food. No paper bags. No plastics. Animals will start digging into your garbage pit almost as soon as you are out of sight. Cans and plastics will not decompose for generations. Used plastic bags can be washed out and reused.

Drop cans and leftover foods into the fire. Smash burned cans flat with a heavy foot, and stuff them into the garbage bag where all junk goes, including the empty butane tank and burned-out batteries. In remote regions, bones and food scraps may be carried well away from camp, out of sight of someone who may come tramping through in a month or two, and left for animals or to rot back into the soil.

Peelings, whether potatoes or oranges, corn husks or leftover vegetables, all decompose and enrich the soil. However, if they cannot be disposed of where they will not be seen, especially citrus peels, either burn them or carry them out in your garbage bag. It's ugly to walk into a site and find fruit rinds and peelings scattered around. Only the thoughtless leave such debris.

It only takes an extra minute or two to leave the campsite clean. Of course the fire is dead out. Scratch through the ashes to make certain

Clean out the cans and nonburnables from a campfire, stamp the cans flat, place all debris in a plastic garbage bag, and take it out with you. Whether you're on foot, on horseback, or riding a bicycle, backpacking, or car camping, cleaning up a campsite is everyone's responsibility.

there are no little goodies, such as pieces of aluminum foil or the lid of a can, left behind.

Who is responsible for camp and fire site cleanup? Everyone who camps there.

In well-used sites, do not scatter leftover firewood. Stack it neatly beside the fire ring, inside a shelter, or underneath a camp table.

THE FINAL INSPECTION

It is essential with any group, especially if there are youngsters, for the last person to leave to make a final check of the complete camp area—look down, for anything lying on the ground; look up, for any garments or gear left hanging on the trees or draped over bushes.

I can still hear the wild shriek from a woman who was on final camp checkup after everyone was packed. As she walked through the area, she found her husband's brand-new sleeping bag hanging on a bush.

Campsite Tips

- Instead of always washing pots and pans with laundry soap and a pad, sometime try scrubbing them clean with sand, pinecones, or both.

- When selecting a campsite near a river check the surrounding land for high water marks indicating past flood levels, then pitch your tents above them.

- For a sturdy pot grabber to lift camp pots and pans without handles, buy the Boy Scout model sold at stores that carry Scout uniforms and equipment. The flimsy ones available at outing goods stores are as unreliable as they are cheap.

- Never take camp stoves or lanterns, whether fueled by gasoline or butane, on a wilderness junket without cleaning and testing them before leaving the house.

- The greatest cause of a sputtering flame on a stove or lantern that uses a wick is a scorched wick. Solution: Cut off the scorched section, or get a new wick.

- If you carry liquid fuel in a container with a screw-on cap, replace the cap with a Super Pour Spout. This will eliminate the need for carrying a funnel.

- If you don't carry a sheet of plastic to put under your tent, in damp or wet weather spread your poncho or plastic bags under your sleeping pad.

- Never leave the camp kitchen when something's boiling on the fire.

- Carry a windup alarm clock. Tired bodies don't always pop awake at sunrise. And a windup won't stop when the battery wears out.

- It will help eliminate moisture from inside a tent to zip open a small crack at the top of one end, and a small crack at the bottom of the other.

- To keep comfy-cozy in cold weather, fill a canteen or plastic bottle with warm water and toss it into your sleeping bag.

- In cold, cold weather, wear your shoes to bed if you need their comfort. But put your feet in a plastic bag.

- Above all, don't go to bed with nothing on but the radio.

9

Camp Cookery and Wild Edibles

Never eat more than you can lift.
—Miss Piggy

Planning Calories for Energy and Nutrition

A critical part of menu planning for any self-propelled wilderness activity is accurately figuring food quantities so every person eats heartily and there is neither waste nor scarcity.

The crucial element is meeting your caloric needs, whether it comes from a vegetarian diet or one based chiefly on protein from meat. Various studies suggest that active adults car camping will devour a minimum of 3,000 calories a day. Paddlers on wilderness rivers, with no more than one moderate portage a day, will wolf down from 3,500 to 4,500. Studies of hikers on the Appalachian Trail indicate that steady trail backpackers will consume from 4,000 to 6,000 calories a day, not including goodies secreted in their backpacks to munch in the security of their tents.

I base the caloric needs for my Sierra Club trips on the recommended amounts in the book *Food for Knapsackers and Other Trail Travelers,* by Hasse Bunnelle, available through the Sierra Club. However, I make these exceptions: For a group of adult men and women, I add 10 percent for trips lasting a week or longer; for teenage males, it is important to increase the amounts by 15 percent.

Two things to keep in mind when planning meals are that carbohydrates provide fast energy, which is quickly burned off on an active outing, and that fats and proteins provide a slower energy that continues to nourish the body long after the carbohydrates are consumed. This suggests morning meals should include some meat and fats for long-lasting energy, and not concentrate exclusively on sugars and carbohydrates, a combination equally necessary for lunches, with perhaps more concentration on energy from fats and proteins. Nourishing packs of high-carbohydrate GORP can be handed out each morning, or a large bag of GORP can be opened at lunch, with whatever else is planned.

In their book *Cooking for Camp and Trail,* coauthors Bunnelle and Sarvis note: "Carefully planned diets contain sufficient quantities of vitamins and minerals for most people, but because cooking destroys vitamin C, supplements of that are advisable on any trip more than a few days long. If there is any question about the nutritional content of your canned or dried foods, add vitamin and mineral supplements."

SIERRA CLUB ESTIMATES

Breakfast

Food	Ounces per person per day	Calories	Comments
Dried fruits	1.5	110	Excellent when eaten dry, mixed with cereal, or simmered.
Cereals: compact cold cereals such as various granolas, Familia, Grape-Nuts, etc.	1.5	150–180	Avoid presugared cereals, or cereals with high sugar content. Sugars add bulk without adding nutritional value.
Instant hot cereals: Quaker Oats, Wheatena, Cream of Wheat, etc.	1.5	150	Some are prepared by simply adding hot water; others must be boiled for a minute or two. Cereals with such extras as raisins, fruits, or flavorings are especially popular. If the cereal does not contain any, add them yourself.

(*Note:* Cereals commercially packaged into individual servings usually contain portions too small for husky camp appetites. Figure on 1½ packages per person.)

Bacon, Spam	1.4	250–300	For long trips, buy the canned varieties. Use the grease for cooking.
Boneless ham or shoulder	1.4	160	Take precooked only.
Eggs	2 per person	170	Whether fresh, freeze dried, or dehydrated, eggs are a breakfast staple.
Potatoes, dehydrated and prepackaged	1.0	150–200	Available in supermarkets; exceptionally popular.
Pancake mixes	2.0	200	Popular, but drags out a breakfast. Reserve for days when you'll be in camp.

Condiments (*)
    Salt
    Pepper
    Basil
    Thyme
    Oregano
    Chili powder
    Curry powder
    Fresh gingerroot
    Tarragon
    Cloves
    Red pepper
    Sesame seeds
    Chervil
    Parsley
    Bouillon cubes
    Garlic or garlic powder
    Rosemary
    Cumin
    Marjoram
    Cinnamon
    Maple flavoring

Based upon your own preference and specific recipes.

Useful if you make your own syrup out of sugar.

(*) plus any others your recipes call for

Coffee, instant	0.15	0	
Tea, instant	0.15	0	
Tea bags	2 bags	0	
Hot chocolate mix	1.0	150	

Nonfat dry milk		100	Buy in prepackaged 1-quart envelopes; figure on 1½ quarts per day per four people.
Flour or biscuit mix			The box will indicate the number of biscuits its contents will make; judge accordingly. Mixes also can be used for thickening instead of ordinary flour.
Sugar	1.0	100	An artificial sweetener will substantially reduce the amount of sugar bulk you must carry.
Dehydrated soup greens	0.1		For enriching many dishes.
Dehydrated onion flakes	0.1		For enriching many dishes.
Dried mushrooms	0.15		Buy dried Chinese mushrooms.
Margarine	1.0	230	Read the label; some require no refrigeration and will keep for several weeks.

Lunch

Crackers, such as RyKrisp	1.5	175	Keep well and are excellent with peanut butter and jelly.
Firm "German" or Westphalian pumpernickel	1.5	100	Also keeps well, but is more likely to be crushed than firm crackers.
Various dry salamis and bolognas	1.5	120–150	Many varieties keep well without refrigeration.
Cheeses	1.5	170	Look for hard cheeses (such as Monterey jack, Swiss, or provolone) or those canned cheeses that do not need refrigeration. On shorter trips, try the canned French cheeses such as Brie and Camembert. Avoid cheeses with unusual and strong flavors.
Tuna fish, salmon, sardines	1.5	125	Canned tuna can be served as is or mixed with mayonnaise or sandwich spread.
Deviled meats	1.5	Varies	Sample at home; some types are quite spicy.
GORP	1.0	220	Use salted nuts or salted soybeans when mixing GORP, especially in hot weather.

Nuts, various	1.0	200	
Peanut butter	1.0	200	A luncheon favorite.
Jelly	0.3	80	To add a touch of something special to the peanut butter.
Candy	0.5	75	Avoid candy that melts.
Dried fruits	1.3	100	Raisins and apples are the most popular.
Powdered drink mixes, including instant iced coffee and tea	Varies		The label will give you the approximate amount per cupful.

Dinner

Soup, dehydrated	Varies		Check on label. Packaged soups specify the servings in either 6- or 8-ounce amounts. Figure on 12 liquid ounces per person.
Sauces and gravy mixes	Varies		Check on label. Usually a package makes an 8-ounce cupful. Popular with almost every starch dish, from mashed potatoes to couscous.
Meat, fresh—steak, boneless	5.0	250	A fine main course the first night in camp.
Fowl, fresh—chicken, turkey	16.0	140	Chickens broil in about 40 minutes; turkey takes much longer. Also best the first night at your put-in.
Canned corned beef, canned roast beef	3.0	200	
Canned ham, boneless	3.0	230	For large groups, buy the meat in No. 10 cans. Quantities and servings are usually clearly specified and accurate.
Canned tuna	3.0	250	
Canned chicken, turkey	3.0	220	
Freeze-dried beef, chops, patties	1.0	130	
Pasta, noodles	3.0	300	
Precooked rice	2.0	200	
Dehydrated mashed potatoes	160		

Dehydrated potato dishes, such as au gratin or scalloped.		210	Servings specified on the label are about 50 percent less than hungry adults will eat in camp.
Couscous, kasha	1.6	160	Serve with a light gravy mix.
Desserts: Jell-O, instant pudding, instant cheese-cake, etc.			Number of servings listed on the package.

Traditional Camp Foods

JERKY

Jerky was first adopted from Native Americans by Spanish explorers. The name itself is from the Spanish word *charqui* for "dried meat."

Ingredients:
   3 pounds lean, inexpensive round steak
   Couple of tablespoons of your choice of dried spices, such as
      herbes de Provence, oregano, basil, or thyme

Directions:
1. Trim all fat from the steak, remove any muscle tissue, and slice along the grain into thin strips ½ to ¾ inch wide.
2. Sprinkle the meat strips with salt and ground white pepper to taste, and the spice or spices you choose.
3. Pound the spices into the meat firmly, but gently.
4. Let stand at room temperature overnight or up to 24 hours.
5. Dip the meat, without stirring, into very hot but not boiling water for 15 seconds.
6. Hang the meat to dry under a hot sun for at least four full days, covering at night to avoid dew, or hang on a rack and place in a 100–130 degree F oven, with the door slightly ajar, for 24 hours.
7. Wrap tightly in plastic bags.

The jerky can be served as is and chewed on like a piece of flavored leather. The thinner the strips, the easier to chew. Or it can be broken into small pieces and added to soups and stews.

PLANKED FISH*

Split and smooth a slab of sweet hardwood two or three inches thick, two feet long, and somewhat wider than the opened fish. Prop it in front of a bed of coals till it is sizzling hot. Split the fish down the back its entire length, but do not cut clear through the belly. Clean, and wipe it quite dry. When plank is hot, spread fish out like an opened book, tack it, skin side down, to the planks and prop before fire. Baste continuously with a bit of pork on a switch held above it. Reverse ends of plank from time to time. If the flesh is flaky when pierced with a fork, it is done. Sprinkle salt and pepper over the fish, moisten with drippings, and serve on the hot plank. No better dish ever was set before an epicure.

To which, after planking fresh-caught fish, I can only add, Amen! Amen! (*The Book of Camping and Woodcraft*, Horace Kephart, 1910)

SMOKED FISH

Caught too many fish to eat in camp, but they'll spoil before you get them home? Rescue them by smoking. Here's one technique similar to the smoking methods of the Inuit:

Gordon's GORP

2 parts raisins, a mix of golden and regular (I often dehydrate green grapes to serve as golden raisins)

2 parts *salted* nuts* (salt helps the body retain fluid during intense physical activity)

1 part M&Ms or similar chocolate tidbits

1 part Cracker Jacks or Japanese rice-cracker nibbles

Anything that looks like I ought to add it

A few bubblegum balls if there are kids along

Hint: If carrying GORP, or anything important, in Ziploc plastic bags, use two. First, fill one bag and seal it, then turn it upside-down and put it into a second bag and seal it for double protection. The bags are reusable.

* Ahoy, nut lovers who munch while hiking across peak and field, now hear this: In a study of 86,000 nurses, it was found that those who ate more than 5 ounces of nuts per week had one-third fewer heart attacks than those who never, or rarely, ate nuts. Dr. Frank Hu of Harvard said despite widespread concern about cholesterol in nuts, the fact is that they do not contain any—regardless of the kind of nuts you put in your GORP.

Cut off the heads, open them from the belly and clean thoroughly, then soak overnight in heavily salted water. Rinse before smoking.

Next—the smoking:

Tie two sturdy cords between two trees, one 6 inches above the other. The lower cord should be about 3 to 4 feet above the ground. Hang a tarp on the higher cord as you would if pitching it for a shelter and stake the four corners reasonably close to the ground, in effect making a steeply sloping roof.

Build a small fire using only hardwood scraps and branches. Hang the fish, butterfly fashion, from the lower cord above the fire. Keep the fire a smoky smudge—the thicker, the better. The heat and the smoke concentrated under the tarp will do the rest. Be careful about letting the fire flare and burn the fish or the tarp. The fish should be smoked for 24 hours, or to taste.

On a hot, sunny day, the fish also can be sun-dried one day, then smoked for 12 to 24 hours the second.

Dehydrated Foods

DRIED MUSHROOMS

There is no need, really there isn't, to toss away money buying delicious dehydrated fungi that you especially enjoy. Dry them yourself. Home drying requires only, the sun, an oven, or, a home dehydrator. Dehydrators are sold by outing goods stores, some health food stores, and the occasional department store.

Do not wash fresh mushrooms; brush off dirt if necessary.

Drying mushrooms:
1. Very small mushrooms may be left whole, but larger mushrooms should be sliced. Some cooks will break off and toss away the stems of larger mushrooms before drying; others may cut the stem into slices for use later for flavoring stews or soups, though they usually are too tough for eating.
2. Spread the slices on a cooking screen or parchment paper and place them in the dehydrator or an oven set between 110 and 130 degrees F, with the door propped slightly open for ventilation. Leave for a minimum of 12 hours, or longer, until the slices are dry and split easily. Turn occasionally while drying.

3. In hot summer weather, the mushroom slices may be placed outdoors in full sunlight for two or three days, turned occasionally, and covered at night to avoid dampness from dew.
4. Whole mushrooms can be loosely strung like pearls from a long string and hung in direct sunlight for several days.

Cooking:

Slices of dried mushrooms may be added directly to soups if they will cook for at least 30 minutes. To rehydrate dried mushrooms, barely cover with warm water and let stand for 30 minutes. The water becomes flavored and can be added to soups or stews. The mushrooms are ready for use in any recipe requiring fresh mushrooms.

HOME DRYING FRUITS, VEGETABLES, AND MEATS

The oven, the sun, or a home dehydrator can be used for drying fruits and vegetables for trail or camp, such as tomatoes, peppers, onions, chives, apples, shallots, carrots, pineapple, or anything else that teases your taste buds. Clean, remove seeds, cut into slices, and dry for 12 to 24 hours in a dehydrator or a 110 to 130 degree F oven with a partly open door for crucial circulation; spread out, or string small slices like pearls, in the hot sun for two or three days.

It usually requires about a half hour to rehydrate them. The water they are soaked in can be added to soups and stews.

Dehydrate canned meats, such as tuna and chicken. This reduces the weight of both the moisture and the can.

Dried fruit slices are delicious. They also can be minced and added to a mixture of nuts for a healthy, satisfying GORP to nibble on during the day.

To make your own fruit or vegetable leathers, choose either naturally tender foods or those that have been softened by cooking, and use a blender, food processor, or food mill to transform them into a smooth paste, adding water if necessary. Spread the paste evenly about ½ inch thick on parchment paper and pop it into the oven at 110 to 130 degrees F, door slightly open, for 12 to 24 hours, or place it in a dehydrator.

Vegetable leathers can be eaten as is or ripped into shreds and added to soups and stews.

Suggestion: Canned tomato paste is ready to turn into tomato leather as it comes from the container.

"INSTANT" PRECOOKED FOODS

Widely available in both supermarkets and health food stores is a steadily increasing variety of lightweight, precooked foods. Like "instant rice," they can be rehydrated and cooked for only a few moments, then are ready to eat. When you next roam the store shelves, pick out one you've never eaten before and try it at home. It may well go on your next trip into the distant woods.

Gordon's Favorite Quickie Menus

Camp cookery needn't be confined to packages of various combinations of precooked freeze-dried and dehydrated foods. Here are a few tasty dishes quickly made in camp. Each serves four to five adults.

GARLIC MASHED POTATOES

6 garlic cloves per each 8 servings of potatoes
Packaged mashed potatoes

1. Cover garlic lightly with water and simmer 10 minutes. Pour off water. Mash garlic.
2. Mix mashed garlic with mashed potatoes.

COUSCOUS

2½ cups fresh chicken stock, or 2½ cups water with 2 chicken bouillon cubes
2 tablespoons dried mushrooms
1 cup couscous

1. Bring stock to a simmer.
2. Add mushrooms and simmer 15 minutes, or until tender.
3. Bring stock to a boil. Remove from heat and add couscous. Stir well and let sit five minutes.
4. Serve promptly. Couscous left sitting any length of time becomes thick.
5. Leftover soup can be served on the side as gravy for couscous.

HUEVOS GORDONOS FOR EIGHT

1 pound bacon

16 fresh eggs or equivalent freeze dried
2 tablespoons milk
2 tablespoons butter or margarine
1 teaspoon herbes de Provence
Tortillas, 2 per person
Salsa

1. Fry bacon until very crisp.
2. Make a large pot of scrambled eggs with milk and butter or margarine, adding herbs to the eggs. Stir constantly so eggs on bottom of pot do not burn.
3. When eggs are ready, heat a tortilla for 30 seconds.
4. Place egg serving on tortilla, add some crisp bacon, and dot lightly with salsa.
5. Roll tortilla and serve.
6. Put salsa on side for those who want spicier eggs.

CORN ON THE COB

Fresh corn, 2 ears per person

1. Strip only outer layers of leaves from corn; remove silk.
2. Bring water to a boil. Add corn. When water returns to a boil, remove pot from heat. Let stand five minutes. Serve with butter or margarine.

BROILED CHICKEN

Chicken, 1 thigh (leg attached) per person

1. Build large fire and let burn down to hot coals.
2. Place chicken on grill over fire and begin broiling.
3. Do not let fire flare up. Sprinkle with water to dampen flame. Flame burns chicken rather than broiling it.
4. Turn frequently for 30 to 40 minutes. Cut into one thigh to make certain it is fully cooked but not dry. Serve.
5. Small pieces of wood can be added to fire while cooking, but be careful about letting it burst into strong flame.
6. Chicken can be lightly patted with butter and sprinkled with a favorite spice before broiling.

TERIYAKI HAM

    Canned ham: 1 pound serves three adults
    Teriyaki sauce for marinade
    Sugar

1. Cut ham into slices.
2. Put ham into Ziploc bag, add teriyaki sauce to cover, and let soak no less than 30 minutes.
3. Broil ham over hot coals—no flame—for three to five minutes.
4. While broiling, brush ham occasionally with teriyaki sauce and sprinkle very lightly with sugar. Serve with instant rice.

Kids Can Cook, Too!

Give hungry youngsters the opportunity to help out with camp cooking. This means more than having them peel the potatoes or set the tableware on a camp table.

For the very young, here are some recipes adapted from Janet Bruno's and Peggy Dakan's booklet, *Cooking in the Classroom.*

PEANUT BUTTER BALLS

    1 cup peanut butter
    1 cup honey
    1½ cups powdered milk

1. Mix peanut butter and honey in a bowl.
2. Add powdered milk and stir until mixture is thick.
3. Roll into little balls. Serve.
4. Clean up and put everything away.

PINEAPPLE FRUIT GARDEN

    1 can sliced pineapple
    1 can fruit cocktail
    Toothpicks

1. Put a pineapple ring on each plate.
2. Stick a piece of fruit on one end of a toothpick, then stick the other in the pineapple. Serve and devour.

CAMP PUDDING

    Instant chocolate pudding
    Tiny marshmallows

1. Make the pudding in a bottle with a screw-on top.
2. Mix thoroughly. Wait until it begins to get firm.
3. Mix in tiny marshmallows.
4. Pour into individual cups. Serve after dinner.
5. Clean up and put everything away.

   For older brothers and sisters, plan foods they can cook, such as the following recipes, for four or five adults.

ABC SOUP

    4 bouillon cubes dissolved in 4 cups warm water
    1 potato, peeled and cut into small pieces
    ½ cup celery, washed and cut into pieces
    ½ cup carrots, washed, scraped, and cut into slices
    2 tablespoons dried onion flakes
    1 cup alphabet noodles

1. Pour bouillon into pot, add potato, celery, carrots, and onion flakes, and simmer 15 minutes. Add more water if necessary.
2. Add noodles and simmer another five minutes, or until noodles and potatoes are tender.
3. Serve and enjoy.
4. Clean up and put everything away.

STIR-FRIED CABBAGE AND CARROTS

    1 small head green cabbage
    1 large carrot
    1 tablespoon olive oil
    1 teaspoon salt
    1 teaspoon sugar
    1 teaspoon sesame oil

1. Slice cabbage into strips as though making coleslaw.
2. Cut carrot into thin strips with vegetable peeler.
3. In large pot, heat olive oil.

4. Stir in cabbage, carrot, salt, sugar, and sesame oil.
5. Stir-fry two to four minutes, or until everything is tender. Serve.
6. Properly dispose of peelings.
7. Clean up and put everything away.

BROCCOLI STEMS

2 cups broccoli stems left after flowerettes are used in other recipes
1 teaspoon salt
1 tablespoon oil
1 tablespoon sesame oil

1. Peel stems with a vegetable peeler, then cut them into thin slices.
2. Sprinkle with salt.
3. In large pot, heat oil and stir-fry broccoli for two minutes, or until tender.
4. Add sesame oil and serve.
5. Properly dispose of peelings.
6. Clean up and put everything away.

Don't hang over older children while they are cooking. Be circumspect. Stand at least 2 feet away.

When planning menus for camp, bring children into the discussion. What do they want to cook over a campfire? Ask their advice for dishes you may not have thought of.

Savoring the Untamed Succory

Let there be no doubt, succory and goosetongue have special uses in the wilderness.

Those who roam field and woods where succory grows in summer abundance, and savor its flavorsome roots, understand why it is cherished by gourmets.

Goosetongue, scattered from city park to ocean beach, is a delight to backpackers who munch its leaves or add them to a salad plucked along the trail.

If you're unfamiliar with succory and goosetongue, you may recognize some of their more common names, such as chicory (*Cichorium* spp.) and plantain (*Plantago* spp.).

A cornucopia of food lies at the fingertips of everyone who roams the American wild lands, from southwestern desert to New England's wooded wonderland. Learn to recognize them. For two significant reasons.

First, many are both unusual and delightfully different foods free for the picking and can be eaten raw, boiled, sautéed, tossed into soups, made into tea, or sliced in salads. Let no outdoor traveler ever again complain at not being able to enjoy free fresh fruits and vegetables on a wilderness trip.

Second, knowing what they are and where they grow can save a lost person from starving to death when nature's rations are as close as a nearby tree, a vine, a cactus, or a root.

Take a Walk on the Wild Side

Edible wild foods can be found wherever you walk, from your own backyard to a city park or distant woodland. Run out of coffee? Then look for chicory. Its roots have been used for generations as an alternative coffee drink. Wild chicory can be recognized by its long stems and the big, showy blue flowers. To enjoy, scrub the roots well, then bake them at 125 degrees F until the stems snap easily. Break the crisp roots into a blender or coffee grinder and grind until they are about the size of your favorite coffee grounds. In your local grocery, the leaves of one species of chicory are sold as curly endive or escarole for garden salads.

Cooking and Serving

It is reasonably certain that in a complex meal of several dishes, something is going to be left somewhere, uncooked and unserved. To reduce this camp tragedy, cooks should place on their worktable *all of the ingredients* for that particular meal. Then start slaving over camp stove or fire.

It will eliminate a lot of fast-grabbing hands if all the food at all meals is served family style. When everything is ready, then invite the famishing to dine. And remember, the campfire and cooking areas are no-smoking zones.

An edible wild plant you needn't hike far to discover is plaintain, with its spadelike leaves. It is about as large as a dandelion. My mother used to tear them up as weeds in her garden. They can be found growing in cracks in the sidewalk, and almost everywhere from Florida to

Chicory

Dandelion

Alaska. Young leaves are tasty in salads; older leaves are cooked like spinach.

Hmmm. You know, young dandelion leaves are also refreshing in a salad at home or in camp.

How to Identify and Enjoy Wild Edibles

You needn't do anything more strenuous than bend over to find some wild, edible plant growing. Consider a few that will enrich your diet and delight your taste buds on your next trip to river or mountain, desert or swamp.

Plantain

The edge of swamps is where cattails (*Typha latifolia*) abound. They are a wilderness supermarket. Carry a basket when shopping. Pull up the roots, scrub, and peel them. They can be eaten raw, baked, boiled briefly, or broiled. On the ends of the rootstock is a small bulb that will be next year's cattail. It is savory raw. In the spring young shoots about 6 to 12 inches long can be yanked up, peeled, and eaten raw or cooked. By the time the shoots are 1 to 2 feet long, they can be peeled and cooked like asparagus. When the

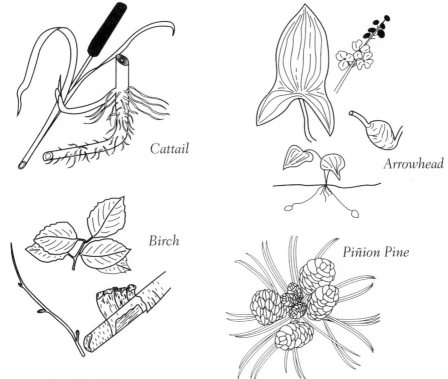

Cattail

Arrowhead

Birch

Piñion Pine

greenish yellow flower spikes appear, they can be husked, boiled, and eaten like corn dripping with butter. Then comes the yellow pollen, as fine as flour. Shake it into a hat and take it back to camp. Use 1 part pollen to 3 parts flour when making pancakes or muffins. Wonderful.

Sunflower

Arrowhead or arrowleaf (*Saggitaria* spp.) is found along the borders of streams and swamps. The arrowhead-shaped leaves may protrude or lie flat. Dig under the water for the edible, small tubers on the roots. Bake or boil like potatoes.

Into the desert: Cacti are a thorny subject. Fleshy stems and branches, peeled of their scales and spines, are edible. The nuts of the piñon, a low-spreading member of the pine family (Pinaceae), are found in the cones; they are delicious when lightly pan-fried or roasted. The trouble is shelling them. Try pliers or a hammer.

We were on an enjoyable late-summer canoe trip in New York's justly famous Adirondack State Park. We had put ashore for the evening. As the cooks were preparing dinner, I spotted a cluster of a mushroom I know well, the shaggy ink-cap *(Coprinus comatus)*.

I plucked a handful.

"Look," I called out rather proudly, "these will taste great in our soup."

I was inundated and shattered by a chorus of no ways, no hows, get those poisonous mushrooms away from our food.

"Okay," I yielded. When the soup was served, I took the pot with what was left, added my mushrooms sliced, simmered the soup briefly, then sat down and guzzled a delicious bowlful. Nothing further was said.

The next morning I heard early risers beginning to make the fire. I poked my head out of my tent. Before I could say a word, two women, eyes flashing, great smiles on their faces, rushed toward me. One grabbed my head and kissed me.

"Oh, God," the other said. "You're alive. We were worried you might have poisoned yourself."

Sweet birch trees *(Betula lenta)* are the camper's friend. The outer bark can be peeled in short strips and is excellent as a fire starter. The thin inner cambium layer is edible raw or cooked.

Both Native Americans and early pioneers stripped the cambium layer from young pine trees to dry and grind up for flour.

A special note: Cutting into the cambium layer may kill trees.

The same watercress *(Nasturtium officinale)* you pick up in bunches at the store grows in thick mats in clear water and springs in the wilds.

Mushrooms are an excellent addition to any meal, if you are dead right in knowing which to pick. You could, otherwise, simply be dead. There are several excellent books for identifying mushrooms. Those with color photographs that include the top, the underside, and the whole fungus, and have either a straightedge or an object of known size, such as a cup, in the background, are the most helpful. Go pick up a book before you pick up a mushroom.

In the spring and early summer, the uncurled fiddleheads of bracken fern *(Pteridium* spp.) are popular at the local market. They are free when you find them growing abundantly in wooded areas. The fern is rather coarse and covered with a hairy felt at the base.

Tea can be made from a variety of plants, but none I've sipped is as pleasant as sassafras tea. Try it. First, find a sassafras tree (*Sassafras albidum*). Simple. It's the only tree with three distinctively shaped leaves, sometimes growing in the same bunch. One is shaped like a catcher's glove, one is a single lobe, and the third is a lobe with two small side lobes. Tear a leaf apart and there is the unmistakable odor of root beer. For tea: Rip up some small roots, scrub them thoroughly, and cut them into small pieces. Use them fresh or let them dry. Put a handful of pieces in a kettle covered with water to make as much tea as you want and let it boil until it turns a nice red color. Sweeten to taste (honey is outstanding). Drink cold or hot. The same root pieces can make tea several times.

The journals of Lewis and Clark reported that Indians in western Montana would dry the seeds of sunflowers (*Helianthus annuus*) and pound them into fine powder. They wrote: "Sometimes they added a portion of water and drank it thus diluted."

Indian potatoes, also known as groundnuts (*Apios americana*), were one of the first wild foods eaten by the nation's settlers. In 1590 Thomas Hariot wrote that they were "a kind of roots of round forme, some of the bigness of walnuts, some far greater, which are found in moist and marish grounds, growing one by another in ropes, or as though they were fastened with a string, being boiled or sodden they were very good meate."

A plant long popular in the Indian subcontinent is purslane (*Portulaca oleracea*), found now throughout the United States and Canada. A ground-hugging plant that is rarely more than 2 inches high, but can be a foot across, its stems, leaves, and flowers are edible. For a salad, pinch off only the leafy tips. Purslane can be eaten raw or chopped and added to soups and stews.

Almost all wild berries with which you are familiar taste even more refreshing on the trail than at home. Look for wild strawberries. Small but sensually delicious. And veteran canoe trip leaders would, if they could, avoid portages when bushes brushing against paddlers' legs are loaded with succulent berries. For this leads to such whining and pleading as:

"Hey, come on, pick up those canoes and forget the berries. We gotta find a campsite. Hey, damnit. Stop stuffing and let's move. Oh well, they do taste great, don't they?"

All camp cereals, biscuits, pancakes, and store-bought puddings are enlivened with freshly picked berries. Blackberries. Blueberries. Juneberries. Serviceberries. Huckleberries. Ah, enjoy them all.

Freshwater Foods

Wilderness lakes and streams are alive with delicious food you can catch without a hook and line.

Freshwater mussels look almost exactly like mussels you get from the seashore. For Moules à la Marinier: In a large pot with a lid, add a cup of dry white wine, minced shallots or onions, a bay leaf, a smidgen of herbes de Provence, and a big glob of butter, or margarine. Boil to reduce the alcohol. Add as many mussels as you gathered, cover, and steam three to five minutes until all shells are open.

For a flavorsome snack, flip over rocks in the water to find crayfish. These cost up to $15 a pound at the fish market.

Frog legs also are expensive, unless they are provided by large swamp frogs.

"Tastes Like Chicken" (Emergency Protein)

No, you don't have to go without meat if lost. Locusts, grasshoppers, crickets, and katydids all are high in food value. You may enjoy them stir-fried.

Grubs and worms and caterpillars can add protein to your wild-vegetable soup. Avoid those with hair or fuzz, which may indicate they are slightly poisonous.

Gut and behead snakes before broiling.

All species of ants, from the tiny red to the large carpenter ants, were widely used by Indians, especially those living in arid regions of the Southwest. They would roast them then grind them into a powder, which was added to a stew cooking over the fire.

To dine on turtles, tear off the shell, clean the sides, and slice up the edible meat. Turtle soup is delicious.

Lily Pads Save Lives

From time to time, stories of surviving under life-threatening circumstances in the wilderness pop up in newspapers. Read them. They are the finest advice you can obtain on how to stay alive in a seemingly hopeless environment. Here is an example:

Lone Man Lost in Woods
Lives Off Lily Pad Roots (*)

MINNEAPOLIS, May 24 (AP)—A 69-year-old North Dakota man survived on lily pad roots for eight days after becoming lost in the dense woods of Minnesota's remote Northwest Angle before a couple found him along a road late Saturday.

The man, John C. Johnson of Pembina, N.D., was taken to a hospital in Roseau, Minn., an hour south of the Angle, which extends east from Manitoba into Lake of the Woods, about 350 miles north of Minneapolis. The area, which is not contiguous with the rest of the state, is accessible by road through Canada or by boat across the lake.

Mr. Johnson endured heavy rainstorms and temperatures as low as 40 degrees at night, clad only in blue jeans, a short-sleeved shirt, baseball cap, red suspenders and running shoes.

"He told me he probably *ate 12 lily pad roots* during the eight days," said his daughter, Jolene Windt of Kokomo, Ind. She said he kept warm by *huddling in hollow stumps and covering himself with bark.*

(*) The *New York Times,* May 25, 1998; emphasis added

Wild Is Clean

To Euell Gibbons, an authority on edible wild plants, the fact that they were not planted by humans was reason enough to dine on them. As he wrote in his book *Stalking the Wild Asparagus:*

The devitalized and days-old produce usually found on your grocer's shelves has been raised in ordinary dirt, manured with God-knows-what, and sprayed with poisons a list of which would read like a textbook on toxicology. They were handled by processors and salespeople and picked over by hordes of customers. By contrast, wild food grows in the clean, uncultivated fields and woods, and has never been touched by human hands until you came along to claim it. No artificial manures, with their possible sources of pollution, have ever been placed around it. Wild food is clean because it has never been dirty.

Wilderness Conservation

Except under emergency survival conditions, protect, do not kill, wilderness wildlife—whether it's a turtle, snake, frog or tree. Build a fire only from fallen branches. Avoid carelessly damaging plants, whether they are growing alongside the trail or the campsite. Be a responsible outdoor conservationist WITH EVERY STEP YOU TAKE.

Camp Cooking Tips

- A friendly nip, with discretion, is a welcome addition on any wilderness outing. Suggestion: Buy overproof rum that can be mixed with water and, for those who wish, a few swishes of powdered drink, such as Tang or lemonade.
- If your meals are made from dehydrated foods, drink extra water to balance body fluids.
- Never take the last drop of soup or eat the last piece of broiled chicken. That doesn't apply to the last sip of wine.
- Plan at least one dish on every trip that you've never eaten before.

10

From Pesky to Perilous:
A Short Course in Health and Safety

A Remedy Against Snake Bite:
If a man procures and eateth rind, which cometh out of paradise, no
venom will damage him. Then said he that wrote this book, "that rind
was hard gotten."
  —The Leech Book of Bald
    c. 900

To Drink, or Not to Drink?

What is the greatest danger you fear drinking directly from spring, stream, or lake in the wilderness?

Since so much attention has been focused on contracting violent diarrhea from *Giardia,* this seems to be the number one enemy. How dangerous is it?

Dr. James A. Wilkerson, author of *Medicine for Mountaineering,* says the microorganism is "not the scourge it has been regarded." In one experiment a group of people was given water deliberately heavily contaminated with *Giardia,* yet "only half" developed an infestation. "Only about a fourth felt any symptoms which, even if totally untreated, disappeared in about 7 to 10 days."

Dr. Gordon Benner, medical adviser to the Sierra Club Outing Committee, tells us to stop worrying about dipping a cup directly into a wilderness lake or river. In an article he wrote for Sierra Club trip leaders, he said: "I admit I do carry a little backup iodine in case my only water source is just downstream from a heavily used campsite. Potable aqua pills are cheap and light, and you can disguise the taste with the powder of your choice (e.g., lemonade, vitamin C, Gatorade).

"But I do love fresh mountain water, and I drink a lot of it, untreated."

As a matter of fact, so do I.

Consider the Source

If you are a wilderness water drinker, it pays to minimize any risk of infection by using your eyes.

Look for a bubbling mountain spring. The chances of sipping a polluted drink are almost nonexistent.

Avoid drinking from water near beaver dams, animal droppings, or any carcass, small or large, lying in the water or on the shore. Go upstream for your water.

Look for water dripping off a snow patch.

Avoid water that is discolored or smells bad.

Walk as far from the shore as far as possible before filling a canteen, bucket, or cup.

Wash Your Hands!

In a national survey of state health departments by the *Journal on Wilderness and Environmental Medicine* made in 1995, it was found that only two cases of giardiasis were traced to backpackers.

The *Journal* added that "giardiasis and similar enteric illness in developed nations are overwhelmingly spread by direct fecal/oral contact or food borne transmission.

"Given the casual approach to personal hygiene that characterizes most backpackers, handwashing is likely to be a much more useful preventive strategy than water disinfection."

The *Journal* report emphasized that campers, canoeists, and hikers should be far more careful with their food on the trail or in camp than at home. Make certain all fruits and vegetables are thoroughly washed and food carefully prepared under the cleanest circumstances possible.

Why Boil Water?

Before you wash the dishes in camp, you naturally fill a large pot with water from the river, bring it to a boil, then wash and rinse. And water for personal canteens is first boiled. After all, if you believe as I once did, boiling water makes it perfectly safe for any use.

However, Dr. William W. Forgey, a trustee of the Wilderness Education Association, fellow of the Explorer's Club and author of such highly respected books as *Wilderness Medicine* and *Essentials of Outdoor First Aid,* says that bringing water to a temperature of "122 degrees F, is adequate to kill all pathogenic organisms," including *Giardia.*

But no matter how long water is boiled, it does not kill dangerous viral pathogens, such as polio and rotovirus. (Why do you imagine the dentist keeps his instruments in an expensive unit that turns water into superheated steam? It would be a lot cheaper to rinse them in a small pot of boiling water if that were effective.)

On the other hand, if you don't have a water thermometer in your kitchen utility bag, go ahead. Boil the water. Then you'll know you have reached 122 degrees F. And guests on your trip won't look askance at your failure to let it boil, let it boil, let it boil.

BOILING POINTS AND ELEVATION

Notice that elevation affects the point at which water boils:

Sea level	212 degrees F
2,000 feet	208 degrees F
5,000 feet	203 degrees F
7,500 feet	198 degrees F
10,000 feet	195 degrees F
15,000 feet	185 degrees F

Do Water Filters Really Help?

For those who fear drinking unboiled water from spring or mountain river, this is the PUR Hiker's model water filter. To reduce buildup of contamination the unit's filter, haul a bucket of water to camp. Let it stand until all debris has settled, then do your pumping.

Widely used, water filters have value—although it may be substantially less for wilderness trekkers than many believe. But there are some situations where a top-quality filter that removes organic chemicals would be a genuine asset. For example, the closer the water source is to farmland, the more likely it could be contaminated by pesticides, herbicides, and fertilizer runoffs. Water in areas of logging, mines, or industrial plants also is suspect.

For the world traveler, a top-quality filter will be of substantial value in a third-world country where there often is little or no treatment of local water. Your filter will save spending American dollars on bottled water every time you want a drink in your hotel room.

How to Select a Water Filter

When filter shopping, be aware that only those that specifically tell buyers they remove organic chemicals actually do so.

Pore size is important in determining what a filter will remove. This dot · is about 500 microns. A filter with a pore size of 4 microns or smaller will remove protozoans, and one of 0.2 microns will remove bacteria. No pore size is capable of removing viruses, which can be as minuscule as 0.00004 microns. Generally, the top-rated filters have a pore size of between 0.2 and 0.3.

Since filter units must be not only cleaned but occasionally replaced, take into account the cost of replacing a filter for the unit you stuff into your pack.

About Altitude Sickness

Altitude sickness is the bane of skiers. But it also can affect anyone engaging in any activity at altitudes above 7,000 feet.

Symptoms usually last only two or three days and are no more serious than tiring more easily and breathing somewhat more heavily than usual.

They can be worse. They can include any or all of the following: unexplained headaches not relieved by medication, lack of appetite, sleeplessness, diarrhea, or nausea. In the most serious cases there may be vomiting, fainting, a loss of sense of balance, and irrational behavior.

Altitude sickness is caused by a complex change in blood chemistry brought on by the shortage of oxygen at higher altitudes. The body produces more red blood corpuscles and more capillaries to carry them. This causes dehydration as the body thickens the blood to improve absorption of oxygen.

Relieving Altitude Sickness

In 1992, doctors doing research with astronomers on Mauna Kea, Hawaii, with an elevation of 13,976 feet, found that a huge increase in water consumption eased splitting headaches in many healthy workers.

They also came up with a breathing technique for cases of disorientation, faintness, or nausea. Take a deep breath and hold your nose and mouth tightly closed while pushing to expel air from the lungs. They said the increased pressure of the air in the lungs is sufficient to drive more oxygen into the bloodstream.

Whether backpacking, peak climbing, or skiing, if severe altitude sickness sets in, try the holding-the-nose technique repeatedly. If that doesn't work, return immediately to a lower elevation.

Avoiding the Altitude Blahs

Can you avoid mountain sickness? Generally, quite easily.

First: If possible, drive from sea-level to high-altitude country over the course of two days. If flying, try spending your first night at a resort or community below 6,000 feet, continuing to a higher elevation the next day. This technique of adjusting gradually to heights is used by mountaineers. Above 10,000 feet, they usually increase the altitude of their base camp by only 1,000 to 2,000 feet each night, no matter how high they may venture during the day.

Second: Avoid dehydration. No alcohol (a diuretic) on the plane, and drink at least 4 ounces of water every hour during the flight. Avoid or minimize alcohol for the first couple of days after arriving by plane at a high altitude.

Third: Drink a minimum of 4 to 6 cups of water daily, in addition to all other liquids, if you will be camping or staying in a ski resort at a base elevation above 7,000 feet. Some authorities recommend that active adults drink 2 quarts of water daily. On my high-mountain adventures we start every lunch and every dinner with soup; the higher the elevation, the larger the bowl.

Climbers have a simple technique to help determine if they are drinking enough liquid: the appearance of their urine. A very light color generally indicates they are getting enough water. A dark color is telling them they are not.

Bee Advised

A bee leaves its stinger in the skin. Remove it with tweezers or fingernails. A wasp leaves only the burn of its sting.

Itches, Stings, and Other Unpleasant Things

On a camping trip in the magnificent White Mountains of New Hampshire, my wife, our four-year-old identical redheaded twin daughters, Hilary and Rebecca, and myself spent our last day on a casual morning walk near a small lake. It had been a fine, long weekend. Weather? As pleasant as every summer day in the mountains should be. We had been bothered only occasionally by a few mosquitoes in the evening. We didn't even bother with repellent on our last, short hike.

As we walked back to our car, one of the young ladies began whimpering and pushing her long red hair aside as she fretfully rubbed her neck.

Mom took a look. "Oh, good heavens. She's all bitten up."

She was. She had a half-dozen red welts on her neck where she had been stung by blackflies.

If it's a scorpion, be careful. Their stings are poisonous and painful—but rarely deadly.

Hurrying to the car, we drove swiftly to the nearest town, and spotted a drugstore; I slammed on the brakes and darted inside. The only person in the store was an elderly druggist at the prescription counter.

"I need some advice," I said as I hurried up to him.

"Yup," he drawled gently.

"What do you do for blackflies?"

He looked at me for a moment, frowned slightly, then, in his New England twang, asked: "Befur or after?"

REPEL 'EM!

Before the days when repellents were sold in every drugstore, campers, hunters, and anglers cooked up their own medicine to keep the stinging, itching, biting insects away.

Here is the "receipt" for one by George "Nessmuk" Sears, an outdoor writer for *Field and Stream* magazine in the late 1800s, and author of the first book ever written in the United States advocating low-impact camping: *Woodcraft*. Published in 1888, it is still in print. Sears's formula:

> Three ounces of pine tar, two ounces castor oil, one ounce pennyroyal oil. Simmer all together over a slow fire, and bottle for use. You will hardly need more than a two-ounce vial full in a season. One ounce has lasted me six weeks in the woods.

Sears's advice on how to use it should appeal to the kid in all of us:

> Rub it in thoroughly and liberally at first, and after you have established a good glaze, a little replenishing from day to day will be sufficient. And don't fool with soap and towels

where insects are plenty. A good safe coat of this varnish grows better the longer it is kept on—and it is cleanly and wholesome. If you get your face or hands crocky or smutty about the camp-fire, wet the corner of your handkerchief and rub it off, not forgetting to apply the varnish at once, wherever you have cleaned it off.

In this cyberspace age, we no longer have to cook up our own "receipts" for repellents. They are as close as the nearest drugstore. They come in a variety of formulas. Pick out any one that works for you. Repellent with DEET is highly potent. It is not recommended for youngsters, because the chemical may be a health hazard to children.

Some campers recommend vitamin B tablets, which, they insist, will change the odor of the skin and repel mosquitoes. Eating fresh garlic has been championed for hundreds of years as an effective repellent— for everything.

HOW TO BUGPROOF YOUR BODY

To reduce the discomfort of getting "eaten alive" by mosquitoes or other insects, wear sturdy fabrics and long-sleeve shirts. A new fleece fabric now is being fashioned into "bugproof" shirts. Even a light neckerchief will protect your neck. Tuck your pants cuff inside the wool or polypro outdoor socks you are wearing to protect your ankles. In heavy mosquito country, avoid sweet sprays, colognes, and aftershave lotion. They are a clarion call to mosquitoes to come and get dinner. Wasps and bees also enjoy the attractive odors.

It is important to spray your socks and pant cuffs, inside your shirt collar, and around your belt, as well as all exposed skin and head, with repellent, both to frustrate such hungry beasties of the air as deerflies and mosquitoes and to keep ticks from crawling around your body looking for a choice place to dine.

In the morning, lay out all your clothes and spray them on the outside with repellent before you dress.

TICK BITS AND BITES

The two most dangerous diseases spread by ticks are Rocky Mountain spotted fever, chiefly in the West, and Lyme disease, which began in the New England region and now is spreading across the nation. Both are treatable with antibiotics. Search children's bodies, as well as the family pooch's and your own, carefully every night, especially the hair, neck, behind the knees, under the arms, and the crotch. Ignore techniques for the "proper way" to remove a tick if its head is tucked into your skin. Quickly, carefully, with tweezers or fingernails, simply pull it out from as close to the skin as possible and dab the area with an antibiotic ointment.

Ticks spread both Lyme disease and Rocky Mountain spotted fever. Insect repellents are effective, but make it a daily ritual to spot-check yourself and your children for trespassers.

PICKING OUT YOUR POISON

The most common source of plant poisoning is from poison ivy. It is almost inevitable that sooner or later everyone is a victim. Reaction to poison ivy varies. Some people are actually immune. Others react almost upon simply seeing it.

There is no need to describe the three-leafed plant. Stare at a color photograph of it in a book on plants until you are absolutely certain you will recognize it the next time you see it. Then stare a little longer to be certain. Also, check out a color photograph of poison sumac, a plant

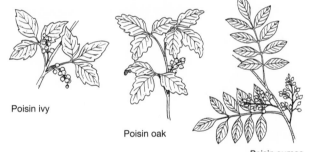

Poisin ivy

Poisin oak

Poisin sumac

Beware of these poisonous plants. Poison ivy and poison oak are actually the same plant, though when it grows as a sort of bush, it's called poison oak. Three shiny leaves a characteristic of the ivy. Both have small white berries in the fall. Poison sumac, with leaf clusters numbering from 7 to 11, grows only as a shrub or tree in low coastal areas.

whose toxin is even stronger and more painful than poison ivy.

RELIEVING STINGS AND ITCHES

The burning pain and violent itch of poison ivy, and the stings and bites of insects, sometimes are relieved by a topical drugstore anesthetic, such as Bactine, or a paste made from baking soda and water, or meat tenderizer. However, when those nostrums fail, try hot water.

Hot water!

Yes, soak a cloth in water as hot as the victim, young or old, can stand. The hotter, the more effective. Apply it for at least five minutes. The itch and pain generally will subside for from four to eight hours. The hot-water treatment even will temporarily stop the damned itching from athlete's foot or crotch rot.

An immediate treatment for poison ivy is to wash the infected skin thoroughly with a strong laundry soap, such as Fels Naphtha, and hot water. When thoroughly washed, there is no danger of the toxin spreading. The blisters are not filled with poison.

HOW TO IDENTIFY POISONOUS SNAKES

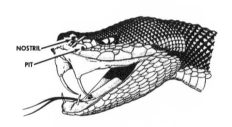

Rattlesnakes can be identified by distinct characteristics front and rear: the head is triangular shaped with pits near the nostrils; on the other end, A RATTLE.

We all have a natural fear of being bitten by a venomous snake. The only four in North America are the coral, with red and yellow bands that touch each other, and the three pit vipers: the rattlesnake, the cottonmouth (sometimes referred to as a water moccasin), and the copperhead. All can be identified by the wedge shape of their heads and the pits under their eyes.

FIRST AID FOR SNAKEBITES

What should you do if you, or a companion, are bitten by one? The surprising answer is: Very little.

Don't bother cutting the bite open and sucking out the blood, or trying to draw off the poison with a snakebite kit. Scientific research has found that whatever poison is injected into the body is spread so swiftly by the flow of blood through veins and arteries that stopping its spread after a few minutes is a hopeless and useless task.

But even more surprising, studies of people who actually have been struck by a poisonous snake in the United States have found that not one in 50,000 died from the venom. For a bite to be deadly, the snake fangs must penetrate deeply and remain in the flesh for a full minute or two. Usually, however, bites are shallow and quick.

One medicine for relieving reactions, given after first gently calming a nervous victim, is Benadryl, or, if you carry it, a prescription antihistamine for reaction to food or insect bites. If there is a severe reaction, get the victim as quickly as possible to professional medical treatment.

PROTECT YOUR EYES

Inadvertently, the crucial necessity of protecting the eyes during outdoor activities is no problem for alpine skiers. They wear ski goggles, which protect eyes from damage caused by a bright sun and from wind.

Unfortunately, most of us who roam the outdoors are often quite satisfied to paddle a canoe, bike a mountain road, or hike hour after hour through the beauty of rolling hills and forests without putting on sunglasses, which are tucked into a pocket or pack.

Barry G. Chaiken, M.D., P.C., a distinguished eye specialist, says continual unprotected exposure can lead to early aging of the eye, which is characterized by growths on the surface of the eye, cataracts, cancer on the delicate eyelids, and wrinkling of the skin around the eye.

Exposure will also cause aging of the macula, bringing on macular degeneration—which leads to blindness.

BE SUNGLASS SAVVY

It is not the color of the lens that is important, but whether the lenses provide almost total protection against the damage caused by invisible UVA and

With the widespread awareness that cataracts may be caused by long-term exposure to the bright sun, summer or winter, the outdoor crowd increasingly shields eyes with sunglasses. To be effective, the lens must protect against UVA and UVB light. The light plastic glasses on this charming lady may not carry an elegant brand name, but they not only thoroughly guard the eyes top, bottom, and sides, but also can be worn alone or over regular glasses.

UVB light rays. Cheap sunglasses may or may not provide any UV protection. The most certain way to ensure that sunglasses offer full UVA and UVB protection is to buy them from a reputable optical shop, or to buy over-the-counter glasses that specifically note on their sales tag that they provide UV protection. Polarized sunglasses also give a welcome protection against reflected glare from water or snow.

Dr. Chaiken's recommendation is for wraparound sunglasses that protect the eyes from the wind as well as the sun.

Lightweight wraparounds are available that can be worn over regular glasses as well as by themselves.

Now, as we say on the trail: "I'll always be seeing you."

The Rule of Three

Whether you're on a trail winding its way through a remote, magnificent forest, or a wilderness waterway, there is, though remote, always a possibility of a serious accident, even for those most skilled and experienced.

This raises the question even before it needs to be asked: What then? Why, getting help, of course.

If the wilderness travelers arranged in advance for someone who knows their course of travel to meet them at a specific time and place, help obviously will be on its way when they don't end their trip at the time planned.

But what if the accident is critical, and life itself depends upon an early rescue?

For the loner on trail or river, the prospects are grim.

For the couple, whether two in a canoe or two carrying packs into the high elevations, not quite as grim. The injured, or sick, waits. The companion rushes for help. The rescue becomes greatly complicated if the sick, or injured, person needs, in effect, bedside help. What does the companion do? Race for help, or stay with the victim?

These are not issues raised on trips that religiously observe the Rule of Three. Three, or more, capable adults on the trail. One hurt. At least one remains with the stricken. Others go for help. On wilderness canoe trips, the Rule of Three is equally important. One canoeist remains with the injured and the canoe, the third paddles like hell for help.

On a backpacking trip, the race for rescue obviously is in the hands, or legs, of the strongest, fastest hikers. On a canoe trip, however, it usually is feasible to put three paddlers in the rescue canoe, which sharply increases the paddling power aboard and the speed at which the canoe can race for help.

The Rule of Three.

Health and Safety Tips

This is a list of helpful ideas and suggestions, some new, some already mentioned, for a trek into the wilds:

- If you haven't done so, take a course in wilderness first aid.
- No candles, matches, or camp stove in a children's tent. Youngsters sometimes light them.
- Giardiasis is spread far more by oral/anal contact than by drinking wilderness water without pumping it through a filter. Wash your hands after a cat-hole trip into the nearby woods.
- Build campfires downwind from the tents.
- Fill the fuel tank before you start cooking with your gasoline stove. Keep an extra cartridge of propane/butane handy. Collect enough wood to cook the whole meal before starting the fire.
- Do not leave a hatchet lying loose on a woodpile. Did you ever see one slammed into a kneecap?
- Teach children how to use a hatchet safely. Let them practice by chopping kindling for the fire.
- Teach children how to use a knife and pass an open knife to another person.

- Never dive or leap into unknown lakes or rivers until you've personally inspected the depth and hazards.
- No food, no candy, no tidbits in tents at night. Animals, enormous or miniature, will come snooping. When it's cold, ignore the rules. Take food into your tent, especially foods high in fat, such as jerky. When you wake up chilled, eat. The energy from the snack will help your body warm up.
- Protect food and the morning kindling from rain and dew by covering everything with a poncho.
- Wear a PFD when canoeing—even in a swamp only 6 inches deep. Carry an extra paddle in each canoe.
- Use a sunscreen with an SPF factor of at least 25 to protect young, and even older, skin from cancer. A sunscreen with moisturizer will help slow the wrinkles of aging, which are amplified by sun and wind.
- When backpacking, skiing, canoeing, wear sunglasses with 100 percent UVA and UVB lenses. They are critical in preventing eyes from developing cataracts.
- Apply insect repellent to clothing to protect the body against ticks infected with Lyme disease or Rocky Mountain spotted fever as well as hungry mosquitoes and deerflies.
- Every inch of every body of every mom, dad, kid, and dog, from hair to toenails, should be checked every night for ticks.
- No one, afoot or afloat, leaves camp without advising someone where they are going, their route, and when they expect to return.
- Don't overpush children on canoeing, backpacking, or biking trips. Know their limitations before you start.
- Everyone on a biking trip must wear a helmet; every bike must carry a warning flag.
- Learn to identify poison ivy before you have to learn how to reduce its sting.
- On wilderness trail hikes, make noise, talk loudly, laugh, but advise nervous animals you are walking through their home territory. Scat!
- Buy only tents with a fabric specifically marked "fire retardant." They will burn. But they will not flash into flame with a single match.

- A few extra items of clothing in a pack will come in handy if there is an unexpected change in the weather.
- Old car batteries sometimes fail when the car is left untouched for as little as a week. If car camping, rev up the engine every couple of days. Before driving off into the wilderness, make sure your trunk has battery cables, a flashlight, a high-lift jack, and chains.
- Carry moleskin for foot blisters.
- Talk to your veterinarian about what your dog may need before taking Tail Wagger on a wilderness canoe or backpacking trip.
- Rocks, leaves, or snowballs may cause major anal infections if used as a substitute for toilet paper. In an emergency, sterilize a rock in hot water for a couple of minutes before taking it to a cat hole.
- Drink plenty of water. An active adult outdoors will need at least 2 more quarts of water a day than an adult at home, summer and winter.
- Always wear latex, never plastic, gloves in treating emergencies that involve blood. For severe bleeding, bind a wound only with a pressure bandage, not a tourniquet, and get professional help swiftly.
- Paper towels are sterile.
- The last thing at night: Inspect the camp to make certain everything is secure. Take the kids with you if they still are awake. When you are satisfied, smile, relax, then everyone off to their tents for a long, pleasant snooze.

11

Knot-Tying Tips and Tricks

*Prayer is indeed good, but while calling on the gods
a man should himself lend a hand.*
   —Hippocrates
      460–377 B.C.

Why Know Your Knots?

Undoubtedly, the first complicated knot most of us learned was the shoelace knot. Remember what a relief it was when you were finally able to tie your own shoelaces? I do. With pride. I knew kids my age who still depended on their mom or kid sister to tie them.

Knowing how to tie the right knot at the right time can be a lifesaver. A few years ago, a teenager got the notion of climbing the rock wall of the Palisades, a stretch of cliff along the Hudson River north of New York City. When halfway up, he slipped and caught himself on a narrow ledge. He cried for help. Some people heard him and rushed to drop him a rope. He grabbed it. They started to pull him up. His hands soon could no longer hold to the rope and he fell to his death.

Had any of his rescuers known how to make the indispensable bowline, he could have slipped a loop around himself and been hauled to safety. Knots are what makes a rope work for you.

Using the Right Knot

CLOVE HITCH

Tying one end of a rope to a tree can be complicated—or it can be no more involved than looping the end of a rope around the tree a cou-

ple of times in a shape known as a clove hitch. Properly tied, it holds under great strain. And it is quite easy to untie.

Consider now a few other knots that you may put into service, wisely and at the right time for the right reason. Look at the illustrations. Practice making them. Not with string but with the same rope you will have with you on your next wilderness outing.

Clove hitch

If you have sons or daughters of Campfire Girl, Girl Scout, or Boy Scout age, they undoubtedly would be proud to help you (re)learn these knots, taking secret delight in becoming your teacher.

BOWLINE

The bowline puts a loop in the end of a rope that will not slip. Quick to tie. Easy to untie. And practical in a dozen situations.

Bowline

BOWLINE ON BIGHT

When you need a loop in the middle of a rope, tie a bowline on a bight. In addition to serving as a loop, the two loops can be spread apart and, if necessary, a person can slip her legs into each loop.

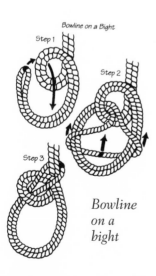

Bowline on a bight

OVERHAND LOOP

The overhand loop can also provide a loop anywhere on a rope. Its disadvantage: When subject to heavy pressure, the overhand is difficult to untie.

Overhand loop

TIMBER HITCH

Send the kids off to find fallen branches for your campfire, and remind them to use the timber hitch to drag their bundle of wood back to camp.

Timber hitch

TAUTLINE HITCH

The tautline hitch slides easily up and down and is amenable to holding tight when it is in place. Great for adjusting tension on the ropes used to keep an old ∧ tent secure.

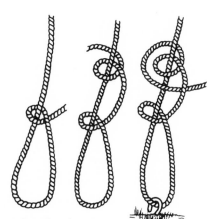

Tautline hitch

PULLEY HITCH

Be cautious when using the pulley hitch to secure a canoe on your car roof to the bumpers. You can double the pressure with this hitch.

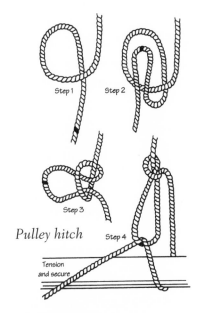

Step 1 Step 2

Step 3

Pulley hitch Step 4

Tension and secure

Sheet bend

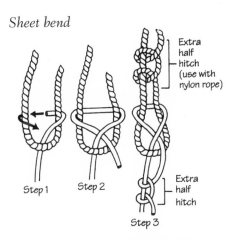

Extra half hitch (use with nylon rope)

Step 1 Step 2

Step 3

Extra half hitch

SHEET BEND

The sheet bend is an excellent knot for tying together two ropes of different sizes. If using kernmantle rope, always secure both ends with an extra half hitch.

Two half hitches

TWO HALF HITCHES

Boaters coming ashore usually tie their bow painter (that is, rope) to a post with two half hitches. Easy to tie. Holds the craft secure while the boaters slip ashore for lunch, or a brief stop.

"Let's tie on one" has no reference to what you do ashore.

Test Yourself

Learning knots by studying pictures of how they are tied is fine. But it doesn't last. Practice does. Tie every knot illustrated. Consider what you would use each for.

Consider some of these problems, and solve them. (The answers are below.)

1. What knot would you use to tie a small cord to a large rope?
2. Which knot makes it easier to pull up a heavy weight?
3. If you want to make a double-loop sling on the end of a rope for a child to use as a swing, which one would you tie?
4. Consider the bowline. It makes a loop that doesn't slip or slide. Can you tie one in the middle of a rope?
5. You want the kids to drag some kindling into camp. How do they tie the bundle of wood together?
6. The rope has to be made longer or shorter to keep something at a tight pitch. What knot?
7. Make the knot that quickly ties one end of a rope to a nearby tree.
8. What do you call one that is even more secure?

Answers: 1. sheet bend; 2. pulley hitch; 3. bowline on bight; 4. yes; 5. timber hitch; 6. tautline hitch; 7. clove hitch; 8. two half hitches.

Epilogue

The clearest way into the Universe
Is through a forest wilderness.
  —*John Muir*
    1838–1914

It had been another long-to-be-remembered canoe trip in the great forests of northwestern Quebec wilderness. In 12 days we had covered more than 130 miles of lakes and rivers in a large looping route that ended back at our put-in.

As we rounded a final point of land I yelled: "There it is. Our takeout."

"Oh, what a beautiful sight," said a cheerful, elderly man paddling bow in the canoe next to mine.

"It is a beautiful country," I heard his partner say.

"Oh it's not the country," he replied, pointing. "There's my car."

Index